Just Brew It!

Beer and Brewing Volume 12

Just Brew It!

The 1992 AHA
National Conference
on Quality Beer and Brewing

Beer and Brewing Volume 12

Edited by Tracy Loysen

 Brewers Publications

Just Brew It!
Beer and Brewing, Vol. 12
Edited by Tracy Loysen
Copyright 1992 by Association of Brewers

ISBN 0-937381-33-0
Printed in the United States of America
10 9 8 7 6 5 4 3 2 1

Published by Brewers Publications
a division of the Association of Brewers
PO Box 1679, Boulder, Colorado 80306 USA
Tel. (303) 447-0816

Direct all inquiries/orders to the above address.

Cover design by Susie Marcus
Conference photos by John Zutz
Photo of Jeff Frane, p. 140, by Elizabeth Actil-Frane
Photo of Martin Lodahl, p. 180, by Ken Buswell

Contents

Acknowledgments

Special thanks to the following companies that assisted financially in the production of this book:

Anheuser-Busch, Inc., *St. Louis, Missouri*

Boston Beer Company, *Boston, Massachusetts*

Coors Brewing Company, *Golden, Colorado*

Fleischmann-Kurth Malting Company, *Minneapolis, Minnesota*

Fromm, Mayer-Bass, Inc., *Yakima, Washington*

Great Western Malting Company, *Vancouver, Washington*

Hopunion U.S.A., Inc., *Yakima, Washington*

Hudepohl-Schoenling Brewing Company, *Cincinnati, Ohio*

Pabst Brewing Company, *Milwaukee, Wisconsin*

Spartanburg Steel Products, Inc., *Spartanburg, South Carolina*

Foreward

Just Brew It! Homebrewers have never been much inclined to assume they can't do something they want to. With each passing year they are inspired to adapt more professional brewing techniques to home use, no longer considering them outside the realm of possibility. In this volume, Steve Daniel takes on the topic of filtering beer, Dave Miller uses his experience at a microbrewery to discuss draft systems, and George Fix outlines means of gaining a near-professional level of control over yeast.

What is even more admirable about homebrewers is that they are not willing to wait for the commercial brewers in this country to do something they can emulate; they take matters into their own hands. Homebrewers explore aspects of beer enjoyment that have virtually no precedent, a phenomenon nowhere more evident than in their penchant for combining beer and food. Candy Schermerhorn seems to generate new recipes for cooking with beer faster than she can write them down. And Fred Eckhardt's understanding of how to appreciate good cheese (by tasting it with beer, of course) surprised and impressed not just his fellow homebrewers but the Wisconsin Milk Marketing Board.

In the realm of brewing, consider how many commercial breweries in this country make Belgian-style beer. One—yet on the homebrew front, there is an entire computer mailing list of folks dedicated to increasing their knowledge of the subject. The lack of commercial interest in these beers means that ready sources for certain essential raw materials (such as yeast and bacteria cultures) are largely lacking, so where do homebrewers get what they need? Incredibly, they have been known to go to Belgium for bottles of fresh beer to bring home and culture up. They just do it, and then they just brew it. "It's as simple as that," says Michael Matucheski, who brewed two Belgian-style commemorative beers for this conference. "Well, maybe not." Just brewing it does not mean that it's easy, just that it is possible.

At this conference, as always, advanced brewers did not forget that they were once beginners, and that there was much to learn on the way to where they are now. In this book, several authors encouraged those who are beginners now to learn more, offering advice on how to improve extract beers, how to hook up with other brewers for inspiration and guidance, and how to otherwise break out of beginning brewing.

Homebrewing is showing a new level of maturity these days. Homebrewers have a growing sense (articulated here by Thom Tomlinson and Steve Fried) that they are the source of much of the best beer in the country and have some of the most finely tuned beer-appreciation skills. Along with this awareness has come a sense of responsibility to keep quality beermaking alive at all levels.

Another indication that homebrewers have come of age is that they are beginning to integrate their collective knowledge. They have always come up with ingenious inventions, new treatises on the biochemistry of the beermaking process, new recipes. The hobby has thrived long enough that there is now a substantial and diverse homebrewing literature. But how does an individual brewer sort through it all, make it fit together? Information is useful only to the extent that brewers can relate what they read to what they actually want to brew. Two authors in this book dedicate themselves to the task of integrating homebrew knowledge in a format that other brewers can easily use. Ray Daniels gives us his insightful analysis of 23 different bock beer recipes, and Doug Henderson explains his computerized HyperCard stack "The Recipe Formulator," which incorporates figures, calculations and conversion formulas gleaned from a wide array of sources.

Homebrewers are concerned about the effects of the current political and moral climate, because it is not particularly friendly to beer. But if this year's conference reflects larger trends in the homebrewing community, then the hobby is in good shape. A healthy, vital group of practitioners is one that encourages innovation; continually pushes the outer limits of knowledge; takes the time and energy to integrate this expanding body of knowledge into coherent, useful systems; and at the same time remains committed to bringing new people into the fold and helping beginners develop their skills. The homebrewing community has all of these characteristics, and more. Perhaps the best sign of health in homebrewing is that its practitioners continue so obviously and in so many ways to enjoy themselves.

Read what the 17 authors presented here have to say about brewing and beer appreciation, then get out there and just brew it!

1. The Legend of Wild and Dirty Rose

Michael Matucheski
Scratch brewer and organic farmer

The 1992 AHA Conference commemorative beers were a labor of love for me, or rather lust, as their names Wild Rose and Dirty Rose might suggest. They were no doubt a little strange-tasting to some of the conference attendees, who certainly wondered, What is this stuff? How does he do it? And why? Well, I just brew it. It's as simple as that. Well, maybe not.

Dirty Rose is the most straightforward of the two beers. She began rather innocently in January of 1990 with a culture of "pure" Rodenbach yeast that my good brewing friend and fellow wild beer aficionado, Mark Kessenich of Madison, had brought back from the brewery the previous spring. He passed it on for safekeeping to Victor Ecimovich, then of Goose Island in Chicago, who gladly traded a slant for a couple bottles of my oakey frambozenbier.

Michael Matucheski

That culture was certainly a lively one. To this day it scares me a little. It crawls with lactobacilli and an odd assortment of yeast strains, whose numbers increase through the ages. I stepped up the culture from a petri dish to a test tube, but most of that culture walked away in a foam, so I had to salvage what was left of the slant by growing the beasties in an old baby bottle until I had enough slurry to pitch into one of my old and trusty 10-gallon oak casks.

By mid-February 1990, I had a 52-gallon oak sherry cask filled with truly foul-smelling stuff, a blend of medicine chest and turpentine. Still, I could pick out something that was vaguely similar to a warm bottle of Rodenbach Grand Cru I had purchased at a Brussels supermarket, being too poor to enjoy the cafe scene. But, since I was due for a spell in Poland, I reasoned a few months of benign neglect couldn't hurt.

I was amazed at the miracle that occurred in my absence. Although still a bit raw upon my return, this murky mix had potential. Later that year, I racked off eight gallons of Rosenbach atop 18 pounds of red raspberries to create the prototype for Dirty Rose, which I "reluctantly" shared at last year's conference in Manchester. A little later I found myself stuffing 105 pounds of raspberries into that cask of sour brown, where they spent the next few months seething and frothing, blowing out bungs and airlocks, and oozing out across my cellar floor.

Wild Rose's origins are a little more obscure. I can trace her roots back to my first attempt at the lambic-gueuze style, something I called Silt Loam Lambic, which was born on December 18, 1987, from five pounds of pale malt, 10 pounds of raw wheat and four ounces of "lambic" Bullions (very old hops). From a simple infusion mash I extracted 10 gallons of wort, which I chilled overnight in the granary, hoping to pick up some house characters. The next morning I racked the wort atop long-dormant cultures of Morte Subite and Lindemans.

Little happened in the next 48 hours, but noticing that the culture jar's dregs had taken off with the addition of some fresh wort, I tossed that into the casks as well, and within hours the barrel was overflowing with foam at the bunghole. Calm was restored about two weeks later, and already I could detect that aroma that is so dear to me, though to my taste much was still lacking—the beer was too bitter, too beery and too thin.

A month later I split that batch between two 10-gallon oak casks and topped them up with fresh wort. I then had plenty to play with, and over the next few years I would bottle off five gallons or so, top the casks off, and run for cover as they frothed uncontrollably.

Still, until February 1989, these lambics were rather limp. Then my guardian brewer, Mark Kessenich, called with word of empty sherry casks waiting for us in Michigan. The next day we were bouncing down the interstate in my old "potato" truck to which we had lashed 15 moldy, slimy, 52-gallon oak barrels still dripping with sherry.

The next week I went on a brewing blitz to fill the first cask with a blend of limp lambic and fresh wort before catching a flight to Poland, hoping to come to my senses. On my return a few months later I noticed that the cask was well-capped with a thick layer of yeast sludge. I racked off a five-gallon sample to bottle. While it was a bit crude yet, there were hints of a cross between Belle-Vue's and De Neve's lambics. I topped off the cask with fresh wort and let it rest over the summer.

By November, a sampling brought back memories of the more obscure village lambics, so I set about to create a frambozen-lambic like the one I had had at the Cantillon brewery in Brussels a few years earlier. I racked eight gallons of my lambic-gueuze atop 24 pounds of red raspberries and let that combination work itself out in one of my 10-gallon casks. A month later I bottled what was to my taste a Cantillon clone, a sure winner. I could see it now—Homebrewer of the Year . . . .

Fat chance. This mother of Wild Rose scored a 16 in the first-round judging. That's categorically undrinkable. I was a little irked, but what do judges know anyway. The suggestion that I use more wheat *malt* proved that. I was happy with my creation. That should have been enough. But it wasn't.

Fate has a clever way of twisting us about, and vindication of sorts came a year later when an obviously desperate AHA conned me into talking at last year's conference in Manchester, N. H., about the strange happenings in my cellar. Somewhere along the way, I recall plying Charlie Papazian, Ray Spangler, Bob Bloom and Greg Noonan with some of my wild ferments, the immediate predecessors of Wild Rose and Dirty Rose. As my ego rapidly expanded, I rattled on about how I had a couple of casks of lambic and sour brown just lying around, as well as a freezer full of raspberries that I didn't know what to do with. Somebody joked about having a lambic commemorative beer for the Milwaukee conference, something about the land of lagers. Why not brew it? So I did. It was that easy. Well, not exactly.

While stuffing 105 pounds of raspberries into a two-inch bung-hole might be a sensual experience for some, the packaging and presentation of these beers was another matter. But, like most of life, it all worked out fairly well in the end. At the very least, I now have an inkling of what most microbrewers go through every day. I still intend to join them. Soon. Very soon.

So here's a breakdown of the specifics for those of you who must have them:

Wild Rose

- 26 pounds pale malt
- 52 pounds raw wheat
- 20 ounces Bullion hops (two to three years old)
  Morte Subite, Lindemans and Antigo lambic-gueuze cultures
- 105 pounds red raspberries

OG 1.050
FG 1.004

Dirty Rose

- 104 pounds pale malt
- 21 pounds crystal malt
- 21 ounces Bullion hops (two to three years old)
       Rodenbach culture
- 105 pounds raspberries (40 percent purple, 60 percent red)

OG 1.060
FG 1.008

Brewing basics:

Infusion mash was at 151 to 153 degrees F (66 to 67 degrees C) for two to three hours. Mashed off at 170 degrees F (76.5 degrees C). Sparged with 173-plus degree F (78.5 degree C) liquor to collect adequate sweet wort. Boiled two hours, with the aged hops added at the start of the boil. Hour hotbreak in kettle. Chilled overnight in the granary, racking to oak casks the following morning.

Cellar temperature averaged 60 degrees F (15.5 degrees C). Raspberries were added after the beers were a few years old, for an additional three to four months of fermentation. All bottles were corked and laid down without prime for approximately six months. All the ingredients were home-raised, of course.

Finally, while I started this madness alone in the wilderness, I have picked up others along the way without whom I can no longer live, nor do I wish to. Many thanks to Mark Kessenich for his prodding over the years (I owe him for the barrels and the rose in the beers); to Bob Drousth for the use of his pump (that setup with its pulsing hoses that pulled creatures from the casks would inspire a potential Dr. Frankenstein); to Dave Norton for donating the corks; to Charlie Papazian, Karen Barela and the AHA staff for tolerating my ranting; and to my true love, Vaughan, for putting up with even worse.

For those of you who had the chance to taste these beers, I hope you enjoyed them. There *will* be more to come.

Michael Matucheski, a contributor to zymurgy, *has been a homebrewer for 16 years and a scratch brewer for the last 12. He hopes to open his own microbrewery that uses only organically-grown ingredients.*

2. A Beer and Cheese Primer

Greg Giorgio
Beer and wine writer

American Homebrewers Association Conferences—let's face it—are about good beer. But for those of us with a creative spark ready to light the flame under another brewkettle, there often glows an anticipating ember of another fire as well. Brewers often love to cook—and combining beer and cheese gives them a way to create uncommon delights.

Milwaukee's rich beer history is complemented well by the wide wonder that is Wisconsin's over 200 varieties of cheese. For the beer and cheese tasting at this year's conference, Wisconsin's Milk Marketing Board sent Betty Buchheit to share six outstanding examples of the Wisconsin dairies' products. Beer accompaniments from some of North America's finest microbreweries stood at the ready.

Candy Schermerhorn, *zymurgy* magazine's "Brewgal Gourmet," conjured beer and cheese recipes. Lucy Saunders,

Greg Giorgio

Top Shelf magazine's food editor, provided tasting tips and beer suggestions. And home-brew raconteur Fred Eckhardt primed tasters with cheese and beer wit and wisdom.

Eckhardt began the session by urging tasters to give their beers a chance up against the fatty, acidic and often palate-coating qualities a stronger cheese may possess. "The heavier beers go better with cheese," he said, then qualified his pronouncement by adding "... and with most kinds of foods." Schermerhorn was quick to offer sound guidelines for cooking with cheese. She suggested being a little less generous with aged, high-fat, fully-flavored cheeses like cheddar, stilton or parmesan when adding them to a recipe. Always melt cheese into any dish slowly, she advised, because rapid heating ruins the creamy texture and turns it stringy. When adding cheese to soups or sauces, remove the pan from the heat and stir gently in one direction until the cheese is incorporated, returning the pan to the burner when necessary to gradually reheat. Salt is a major component of cheese, so taste foods after it has been added. Be particularly wary of overbrowning cheese under the broiler—try for a bubbly and golden look rather than black-ened and rubbery. Once cheese has been opened, store it tightly wrapped in clear plastic, using fresh wrap with each use. Trim mold from hard cheeses and re-wrap. Moldy soft cheeses have seen their best; throw them away.

All this talk of cheese gets a mouth to salivating, which

brings me to the first beer and cheese combination. This offering matched the hoppy Anchor Steam Beer with the mellow, mildly buttery and semi-soft Butterkäse.

"Warm it gently in your hand," Lucy Saunders suggested, to allow the fullness of the cheese's aroma and flavor to develop. Saunders and the rest of the panel wanted everyone to think about the aroma, flavor, and textural profile of the cheeses as much as they considered those of the beers offered with them.

Anchor Steam has the full, malty body and firm, sharp Northern Brewer hop palate of an ale, but is subtly less fruity. The hops neutralized the gentle, nutty/buttery flavors in the Butterkäse, and brought out some fruity alelike notes from the beer. Hops predominated in the aftertaste. Schermerhorn yearned for a puff pastry, baked to a golden brown. It would be filled with mushrooms, onions and herbs, sautéed in butter and Steam Beer, then wrapped in Butterkäse. Another idea was a risotto with onions sautéed in beer, and the cheese stirred in to thicken before serving.

Havarti, Wisconsin style, is usually firmer in body than its European counterpart. This medium-flavor, buttery, tangy cheese was a nice blend of flavors with Milwaukee's Sprecher Weiss. Fruity, tart and yeasty Weiss flavors and the buttery tang of the havarti enhanced each other impressively. How about a havarti and mushroom salad dressed with Specher or other Weiss beers and nutty walnut oil? Schermerhorn's "Classic Wisconsin Combination"—a baked tart of sliced potatoes and ham, sprinkled with havarti and Weiss—sounded good to many tasters. Fire up the oven!

"You can enjoy these things without overdoing them," Eckhardt announced as attendees rolled their eyes in reaction to the fat-laden tart. Employing a classic, "relax, don't worry" argument, he called for simple moderation in all areas of good

Lucy Saunders, Fred Eckhardt and Candy Schermerhorn (left to right) educate homebrewers on the subtleties of combining beer and cheese.

food and drink. "If you spend your life worrying about cholesterol, you'll be worrying about cholesterol and die anyway."

The next combination featured fontina and Hart Brewing's (Carleton, Ontario) Amber ale. Fontina is a semi-soft, delicately flavored cheese, great for sauces and fondues, easily enhanced by beer. The slight earth hint in the fontina gave itself willingly to the grainy, malty palate of the Hart Amber, turning nutty, with spicy hops dressing up the finish. Saunders saw the sometimes nutty, grainy character in ales working well with more than just a fontina. Schermerhorn enticed the audience with the idea of a Hart Amber bread dough filled with fontina, sautéed onions and roasted peppers. Suggestions for pizza, pasta, and sauces for vegetables and potatoes were forthcoming as well.

It was probably a toss-up for favorite cheese honors here, but the Bavarian-style, blue-veined brie certainly garnered its share of supporters. Eckhardt was very pleased with the cheese's flavor and origins, which are somewhat removed from the classical: "It's nice to know even an aged style of cheese can be modified and updated."

The brie and Lakefront's East Side Dark were meant for each other. Complex, oily, bitter mold flavors, and salty, creamy elements in the cheese were rounded by the malty, meaty flavors in this Klisch brothers' classic Milwaukee brew. Schermerhorn's suggestion of turnovers, stuffed with brie and apples and seasoned with this beer sounded like divine intervention at this juncture. She went on. What about brie buttermilk biscuits, mixed with beer, or brie and toasted pecans stuffed into dates? "Is this stuff good, or is this stuff good?" Schermerhorn didn't have to wait for the applause.

"Wait 'til you sink your teeth into this one," Eckhardt said with a sly grin. It was a three-year-old block of absolutely toothy cheddar, drying and crumbly, with an almost crunchy sharpness to the taste and texture. "Outrageous," one nearly overwhelmed homebrewer exclaimed, tasting the cheese while sipping the full-flavored Red Feather Pale Ale from Chambersburg Brewing Company in Pennsylvania. As hoppy and full-bodied as this ale is, the cheddar's nutty, tart/sweet combination of flavors nearly overwhelmed it. This was a subtler mix that gave a little extra sweet, buttery edge to the cheese. The "Brewgal" couldn't resist a hint for green chilies stuffed with cheddar, sour cream and toasted almonds, baked and cloaked with Red Feather sauce.

Saunders cited one of cheddar's special attributes, its cavity-fighting ability. Also, its high calcium content is utilized more easily than is the calcium in milk. And Eckhardt will tell you about beers "lupulin effect," which helps you breathe deeply, sleep more soundly, and sing better. There was some music still to come.

Gorgonzola is another aged style—a pungent, veined, cured blue-type cheese that is often milder than other blues. The Wisconsin example in this tasting was very buttery and salty, with a subtle mold bitterness that sang its own tune with hoppy harmony from Anchor Porter. The beer's smoky, licorice, roasted characteristics and its rich hop flavors were even more pronounced with a backing of Gorgonzola. This match reaffirmed Saunders' belief that the veined cheeses are fine pairings with roasted, smoky, dark ales, in much the same way that these cheeses work with late-harvest, botrytis-influenced wines.

Schermerhorn was reeling off ideas fast and furiously now: salad dressing with Anchor Porter, Gorgonzola, oil, garlic, and thyme; pears poached in porter and honey, stuffed with Gorgonzola and toasted walnuts.

The room was boppin'.

All the predetermined beer-and-cheese combinations having been tasted, homebrewers began improvising new combinations at their tables. Some stated preferences for beers with wilder, yeasty components, including acidic lambics, as companions to the assertive flavors of aged and moldy cheeses. This was obviously a crowd in tune with beer and cheese. Eckhardt called for more research. Cheeses, which are fermented food, are highly variable within a stated style. "Know your cheeses as you do beers. Experiment," Eckhardt said. Know that slightly ammoniated rinds, bitterness and astringency are all common elements of classic cheeses. "The bark is worse than the bite," Saunders offered, optimistic that people would be tasting more widely in the future.

A round of applause for the cheeses and beers signalled the end of a session, and perhaps the beginning of a new kind of enjoyment for us. Schermerhorn is a longtime lover of beer and cheese, but hadn't really known the extent of what Milwaukee could offer. And Betty Buchheit, who often pairs the fine cheeses of Wisconsin with wines, was duly impressed— so much so that she is preparing a Wisconsin Milk Marketing Board guide to beer and cheese. "This tasting really opened my eyes."

Greg Giorgio, a freelance beer and wine writer from Altamont, New York, has been a homebrewer and AHA member for five years. A certified beer judge, Giorgio enjoys the hoppy bite of English ales and the exotic range of Belgian brews, and makes the occasional smoked chili beer, lambic-style ale and melomel.

3. Beer and Brewing in the 21st Century

Steven J. Fried
Brewer, McGuire's Irish Pub, Pensacola, Florida

I started homebrewing in 1979 and, as a relative old timer, I am pleased with and excited about the growth and enthusiasm in our hobby today. But as fast as homebrewing has grown and changed over the last 13 years, I believe that in the next few years this trend will accelerate—not only in homebrewing but in microbrewing as well. Moreover, the American public's image of beer will change. The words that come to mind are respect and acknowledgement of a distinctly American higher art form. The many styles of beer, and the general knowledge of the brewing process that is second nature only to homebrewers and those in the business, will become mainstream in our culture. And when historians look back to chronicle the beginnings of the New Age of American Beer, they'll find the American Homebrewers Association.

Steven J. Fried

Modern homebrewing rose out of the rubble of hundreds of small and regional breweries bulldozed by the national giants following the repeal of Prohibition. By the 1970s, beer had become a commodity in the United States like sugar, flour or bean dip. But people like Charlie Papazian, Fred Eckhardt and Byron Burch, upon surveying this vast beer wasteland, were not satisfied. These were the stubborn innovators who thought, "If I can't buy the kind of beer I want, by God, I'll make it myself." In this way, the homebrewing movement was born. It in turn gave rise to microbrewing 10 years ago, and look how fast that has taken off. Where is it all going?

Before we look into the future, what of the present? An obstacle that concerns me greatly is neo-prohibitionism and the threat it poses to us all. The elitist, paternalistic, anti-alcohol crowd in and outside our government is targeting brewers and consumers with taxes, regulations and media pressure in order to reduce consumption. The new government warning labels and attacks on beer advertising are portents of things to come. The public is being subjected to a misinformation campaign designed to portray any alcohol consumption as socially and personally destructive behavior. Much of the campaign is aimed at our children, who learn in grade school to equate legal alcohol with illegal hard drugs. A stigma has been attached to alcohol consumption in this country that doesn't exist in many others. Germany and Japan, for example, have harsh laws on drunken driving, yet alcoholic beverages play an important and repected role in their culture. Why not in the United States? We as small-scale brewers may help effect a change in current attitudes because of the emphasis we place on quality, not quantity, in our beer drinking. About the only positive press beer gets these days is from stories on homebrewing and microbrewing. Therefore, we have a collective responsibility to maintain an image of quality and moderation. This can be done through promotion of our meetings, tastings, festivals and other community events. More importantly, we must grow—and growth, in my opinion, hinges on homebrew clubs.

The AHA estimates that there are now 1.5 million homebrewers in this country. Many are finding information, camaraderie and fulfillment in homebrew clubs. Club meetings and the national homebrew conference are fantastic forums where ideas are exchanged and the hobby as a whole is advanced. In my own case, I made typical malt extract homebrews for years, as did our local homebrew club members. No one was particularly interested in investing the time and money in a first-class, all-grain, draft system. Then, two years ago, while I was working at McGuire's, a customer visited the brewery and caught the homebrew bug bad. Within a year his brewing expertise had surpassed that of the other long-time homebrewers, who were still knocking around with extract, dry yeast and bottles. And then a fascinating thing happened. Everyone else wanted to improve, too, once they saw how easily all-grain, draft homebrew could be made and how much better the results could be. Quality brewing is truly infectious.

The future of homebrewing will see continued improvement in equipment, brewing technique and yeast. In the interest of exchanging information, I would like to pass on some ideas that I believe will help you make better beer. Some of them are fairly unconventional, and you may be as reluctant to accept them as I was when I was first trained to brew commercially. My overall advice is to keep it simple. Recognize that you can't do it all but that you can make good commercial-quality beer, consistently and with minimum trouble, with an investment of under $1,000.

If I were to take up homebrewing again, I'd go with a 10-gallon stainless all-grain system fashioned from scrap 15 1/2-gallon beer kegs. You can buy a system off the shelf, or you can take your plans to a local welder with stainless experience and have a system made to your specifications. I suggest a simple single-step infusion mash/lauter tun system. It doesn't require continuous stirring, heating or temperature monitoring. Just mix a measured amount of grist at room temperature with the proper amount of strike water at 168 degrees F (75.5 degrees C) to yield a mash-in temperature of 154 degrees F (67.5 degrees C). I sparge after one and a half hours and add Irish moss to the boil to take care of the chill haze. A propane gas fish cooker makes an excellent heat source for the boil. A small pump with a valved output is the best way to transfer wort through a heat exchanger or beer through a filter. Using an old refrigerator with a temperature controller, ferment between 55 and 65 degrees F (13 and 18.5 degrees C) in stainless or glass fermenters. When final gravity is reached, cool down to 32 degrees F (0 degrees C), and transfer or filter into soda/beer kegs. Carbonate by sending CO_2 through the dip tube, shaking the keg occasionally to dissolve the CO_2 under 15 psi head pressure. Modify another old refrigerator to use as a beer keg cooler and draft system by attaching beer faucets through holes drilled in the side. In Pensacola, we have a local company that supplies soda system parts and sells all the materials needed for a draft system using soda kegs.

The Mad Scientist, alias Steve Casselman, challenged conference attendees to let their minds run free and expand the boundaries of homebrewing.

For cleaning vessels and related equipment, I use warm water, Dawn dishwashing detergent (it rinses clean) and a scrub pad. A caustic cleaner such as a sodium hydroxide or a potassium hydroxide solution (used by breweries and commercial dishwashers) is useful in removing scale from stainless steel, but precautions must be taken; i.e., wear rubber gloves. For sanitizing, I use hot water at 180 degrees F (82 degrees C) for 20 minutes or an iodophor solution for five minutes. I sanitize all equipment and fittings that come into contact with cooled wort or beer.

Selection and care of your yeast should be your highest priority. I use an alt strain and have been repitching this yeast successfully for over three years and 400 generations. I have never washed or recultured it. I believe homebrewers can learn from my experience. If you have the equipment and technique to brew clean beer, if you use a clean strain of yeast resistant to genetic degradation, and if you brew regularly, then you can reuse your yeast indefinitely. The catch is that once the yeast is cropped and placed in the refrigerator, it has a shelf life of 10 to 14 days without restarting.

I have a philosophy about beer styles, recipes and good beer. If you follow a sound brewing system, any reasonable recipe will produce good beer. By good beer I mean a beer that tastes so good you want another. Once you have a system and a yeast, stick with them while varying ingredients, as opposed to bouncing back between ales and lagers and other complex mashing and fermenting schemes. I have felt sorry for new homebrewers who jump right into advanced recipes or lagering only to be disappointed after all their effort. Remember—the first goal is good, drinkable beer, not nirvana from having brewed every beer style known to the civilized world.

By the year 2000, the homebrewers in this country will be making some fine beer, on a par with any commercially made beer in the world. I predict that with this narrowing of the quality differential, the term homebrewer will eventually give way to the term "amateur brewer." Then, as the success of microbreweries and brewpubs continues to spread, more and more of our homegrown amateurs will find business and employment opportunities in the microbrewing industry. There were once 4,000 breweries in this country; who's to say it can't happen again? The market is either there or soon will be, but who will be qualified to do the brewing? Professional brewmasters are too few in number and probably wouldn't be attracted to the low pay, hard work and long hours. I guess that leaves you.

Steve Fried has been brewing beer at McGuire's Irish Pub in Pensacola, Florida, since the installation of the brewery in 1989. For 10 years prior to that, he was a dedicated extract homebrewer.

4. Cooking with Beer

Candy Schermerhorn
Culinary instructor, consultant and author

Combining the complex qualities of food and beer when cooking can be as stimulating and diverse as uniting distinctive malts and hops when brewing. Customizing a beer's very essence to your own individual tastes is a rewarding, creative process. Cooking with beer is an extension of this process. Investigating the endless combinations of beer and food allows brewers to further glorify the results of their brewing prowess. Homebrewers routinely examine the overall quality of their beer, checking for head retention, clarity, flavor, etc. When cooking with beer, the homebrewer extends this evaluation to include an assessment of which foods would benefit from the character of that particular beer.

The book *Brew Free or Die*, which recounts the 1991 AHA National Homebrew Conference in Manchester, New Hampshire, includes an in-depth discussion of the mechanics of

Candy Schermerhorn

cooking with beer (Schermer-horn, 1991). Rather than re-peat the information included in *Brew Free or Die* on the fun-damentals of cooking with beer, the emphasis here is on recipes that integrate food with the celebrated beer styles of the world. Determining which recipes would best ex-press the spirit of the 1992 Conference in Milwaukee was a matter of region. It seemed fitting that the recipes should focus on Wisconsin's pictur-esque dairies, lush farmland, superb beers and warmhearted, generous populace.

When it comes to cooking with beer, I am always asked, "What is the most important rule of combining beer and cooking?" My response is this: *always recognize that the beer should enhance and enrich the flavor of the ingredients used, not conceal them.* Many people think of cooking with beer as simply boiling ribs in four quarts of beer. On the contrary, cooking with beer is akin to cooking with wine. It should be light-handed and discreet, the subtlety of the beer peeking out amidst the flavors of the food.

Many recipes may require only a few tablespoons of beer to augment their flavor. The amount of beer required in a recipe is not important. How the beer transforms the flavor of the dish, heightening and enhancing the final qualities, should be of greater concern.

Another often posed question on cooking with beer is, "What type of beer should I use?" There are hundreds of

Candy Schermerhorn (right), with AOB marketing director Matt Walles and another helper, preparing Beerish Meatballs and truffles for her conference presentations.

classic beer styles to choose from and infinite palates to please. The styles used in my recipes reflect personal preferences gleaned from extensive sampling and research.

Keep in mind that personal preference, budget and availability will greatly influence the type of beer you use in your cooking. Do not avoid a recipe because the beer style called for is not available; simply use a style that would be a compatible substitute. The basic rule—never overshadow the dish with your beer—can guide you through most decisions on choosing the beer for a recipe. Traditionally, you would not add stout to chicken-and-rice soup or a white chocolate mousse. Neither would you add a sparkling cider to a heavy, dark rye bread, for the cider's flavor would be lost amidst the intensity of the rye.

Those all-important basic recipes that guided you through your first batches of beer were treasured for giving you a start with your brewing escapades. Let the following recipes serve you in the same manner. They should merely provide the guidelines for those first adventures in cooking with beer. Do not forego a dish because it uses too much pepper, herbs, cream, etc. Recipes are meant to be customized and adjusted to fit your own tastes. Use your imagination and creativity. Cooking with beer is the kissing-cousin to brewing the beer. Both should result in a superior flavor that is distinctive and personal.

BREADS

Bread and beer of every type have sustained humankind throughout the ages. The varieties and flavors of each are as endless as the possibilities of combining them in cooking. The following beer-enhanced recipes include a sampling of quick breads, yeast breads and a delightful Belgian waffle.

Quick Breads

Quick breads are leavened with baking soda or powder. Enriching them with beer augments the tender texture and flavor of these timeless favorites.

A few hints for tender quick breads:
- Handle the batter as little as possible.

• Combine the dry ingredients in one bowl, wet ingredients in another bowl before mixing them together.

• Stir batter until just moistened. Small lumps disappear during baking.

Savory Scones

Scones are rich biscuits that can be sweet or savory. This recipe incorporates bits of cheese and beer-soaked ham for a hearty biscuit. Makes 10 to 12.

        1/2 cup quality ham, diced finely
          3 tablespoons Belgian ale (for soaking ham)
          2 cups all-purpose flour
          1 tablespoon sugar
          2 teaspoons baking powder
          1 teaspoon dried herbs (thyme, savory, dill, etc.)
        1/4 teaspoon salt
          8 tablespoons butter
        2/3 cup grated Gruyere or Swiss cheese
          1 extra large egg, beaten
          3 tablespoons Belgian ale
          3 tablespoons light cream or milk

Combine the ham and 3 tablespoons of ale in a heatproof container and heat until hot. Cover and let stand for 15 to 30 minutes. In a medium bowl stir together the flour, sugar, baking powder, herbs and salt. Cut in the butter until crumbly and then stir in the cheese. Beat the egg, ale and cream together. Make a well in the dry ingredients and add the egg mixture and soaked ham. Stir gently to distribute the moisture until the batter clings together in a ball. Knead gently for 5 to 8 strokes. Roll or pat into a 3/4-inch thickness.

Using a 2-inch biscuit cutter, cut into the desired shape, dipping the cutter in flour between cuts when necessary.

Place on an ungreased baking sheet and bake on the center shelf of a 400-degree oven for 12 to 15 minutes or until pale gold on top. Serve immediately with fresh butter.

These scones can be frozen raw once they are cut. Separate them with waxed paper or plastic wrap and store them in an airtight container. To bake, place frozen scones on a baking sheet and bake 15 to 17 minutes.

Marvelous Corn Muffins

These moist muffins are bursting with Midwestern corn flavor.

```
   1   cup yellow corn meal
1 1/4  cups unbleached flour
 1/2   cup sugar (less if using canned creamed corn)
   2   teaspoons baking powder, sifted
 1/2   teaspoon baking soda, sifted
 1/2   teaspoon salt
   1   egg
 1/4   cup oil
   1   cup fresh cut corn run through a blender, or creamed
 1/2   cup India pale ale*
 1/4   cup powdered milk
```

* The liquid content of the corn will affect the amount of beer needed. Use the amount called for and if the batter seems dry, add an additional 2 tablespoons of beer.

Preheat oven to 375 degrees. Generously grease 12 standard muffin tins. Place the cornmeal, flour, sugar, baking powder, soda and salt in a large bowl and whisk until combined. Put the egg, oil, corn, beer and powdered milk in another bowl and beat until thoroughly mixed.

Combine the wet and dry ingredients, stirring just until all the ingredients are moistened. Spoon into the prepared tins, filling them three-quarters full. Bake until the muffins are springy to the touch and golden brown.

Yeast Breads

Yeast breads prepared with beer are extremely flavorful and tender. For a detailed explanation of the process of making yeast breads, see the "Breads" section in Schermerhorn (1991).

It is important to use bread flour that is high in gluten, the substance in flour that makes dough elastic. The gluten-formed structure traps the carbon dioxide bubbles released by the yeast, thereby raising the dough. It also is important to knead the dough thoroughly to strengthen the gluten-formed structure, so that it will not rupture and deflate while baking.

Black Rye Bread

Lush with the flavor of rye, stout and cocoa, this peasant-style bread is an Old World indulgence when served with slabs of cured ham, country-style cheese, sliced onions and fresh radishes dipped in salt. What a memorable feast!

    2 cups dark bock or stout, warmed to 110 degrees
    2 tablespoons yeast
    4 tablespoons butter, melted
    2 eggs

     1/2   cup honey
       3   tablespoons caraway seed
     1/4   cup cocoa powder
       1   tablespoon salt
       4   cups medium or dark rye flour
 3 to 4   cups bread flour
       1   egg white mixed with 2 tablespoons warm honey

Place one cup of the rye flour in a large bowl and stir in the dry yeast. Pour the warm beer over the mixture, whisking thoroughly. Cover and allow the mixture to rest in a warm spot for 15 to 20 minutes.

Stir the butter, eggs, honey, caraway, cocoa and salt into the yeast mixture, whisking until well combined. Stir in the remaining rye flour 1 cup at a time. Stir in the bread flour 1 cup at a time, using your hand when the dough becomes too heavy for a spatula. Continue adding flour until the dough begins to pull away from the bowl and kneading can begin. Knead the dough vigorously, adding only enough flour to prevent the dough from sticking.

When the dough is smooth and elastic, rub the inside of a large bowl with a scant tablespoon of vegetable oil. Press the dough into the bowl and turn it over, coating the entire surface of the dough with the oil. Cover the dough and allow it to rise in a warm spot until doubled, usually 2 hours. When the dough has doubled in bulk, punch it down, divide it in half and allow it to rest for 5 minutes, covered.

Roll the dough into firm round or oblong peasant loaves. Place the loaves on parchment paper, cover and allow to rise until doubled. Brush the tops with the egg white and honey. Lightly score the tops with a sharp, serrated knife. Bake in a preheated 350-degree oven for 30 to 35 minutes, until the tops are darkly glazed and the bottoms are well browned.

Potato Bread

Beer and potatoes are teamed in a delectable loaf, enhanced even further with fresh dill. This bread was formed into dinner rolls and served at the Conference Grand Banquet.

```
        2  large baking potatoes, peeled and cubed
        1  cup potato water
        1  cup India pale ale or Bavarian light lager, warmed
      1/2  cup powdered milk
        2  tablespoons dry yeast
        3  tablespoons sugar
        4  tablespoons oil
        1  tablespoon dried dill or 3 tablespoons chopped
              fresh dill
6 to 6 1/2  cups bread flour
   2 to 3  tablespoons milk
```

In a covered saucepan, simmer the cubed potatoes in enough water to cover until very tender. With a slotted spoon, remove the potatoes and set aside. Cool the liquid to 110 degrees. In a separate bowl, combine the yeast with 1 cup of the bread flour. Whisk in the cup of potato liquid, beer and powdered milk. Allow to sit 15 to 20 minutes.

Mash the potato chunks and add them, along with the sugar, oil and dill to the yeast mixture. Follow the directions in the Black Rye Bread recipe for mixing, kneading, and letting the dough rise.

Form into loaves and place in greased loaf pans. Cover and allow to double. Immediately before placing the loaves in the oven, brush each loaf with milk. Bake until pale gold on top and bottom. Cool before wrapping in plastic.

This bread makes fabulous hamburger buns too!

Yeast-Raised Belgian Waffles

Light and ethereal, these yeasty waffles are much more than just breakfast fare. Try them as a base for fresh fruit topped with whipped cream or ice cream sundaes.

      3 cups unbleached flour
      1 tablespoon bread yeast
  1 1/2 cups warm water (110 degrees)
  1 1/2 cups warm Oktoberfest beer
    1/2 cup sugar
      2 large eggs
    1/2 teaspoon salt
      6 tablespoons melted butter
    1/4 cup vegetable oil
      1 teaspoon vanilla extract

Stir 1 cup of flour with the tablespoon of yeast. Whisk in the warmed water and beer. Cover and place in a warm spot for 15 minutes. Beat the sugar, eggs and salt until lemon colored and fluffy. In a separate bowl stir together the butter, oil and vanilla. Combine all the ingredients and beat for 2 minutes. Cover and refrigerate from 4 hours to overnight.

Stir down the batter and cook in a generously greased Belgian waffle maker until crisp and brown. Serve immediately or cool on a rack before storing in an air-tight container.

Try these with the Sweet Beer Sauce on page 56 for an eye-opening beer-enhanced breakfast.

POULTRY

Beer is a perfect medium for reinforcing the flavor of poultry dishes. From basic to complex dishes, poultry seems to revel in the flavor of beer.

Pilsenered Chicken Breasts

These beer-imbued breasts are really given the Pilsener treatment. They are first marinated in Pilsener, then stuffed with ham, cheese and Beer Mustard, and finally served with a Pilsener Sauce. Irresistible! Serves four.

        1   cup German Pilsener
    1/4   cup olive oil
            juice of 1 lime
        1   clove garlic, minced and mashed
        2   teaspoons tarragon
        2   whole chicken breasts, split, skinned and boned
        4   slices of Black Forest ham, each 3 x 2 inches
        4   thick slices of Gruyere, each 3 x 1 inches
        1   tablespoon Sweet-and-Hot Beer Mustard (see recipe
              on page 56)
    1/2   cup flour
    1/2   teaspoon salt
    1/4   teaspoon freshly ground black pepper
    1/4   teaspoon paprika
    1/8   teaspoon cayenne pepper
    1/3   cup buttermilk
        1   stick unsalted butter

Combine the beer, olive oil, lime juice, garlic and tarragon and allow to stand while the chicken is being prepared.

Form an unbroken pocket in the breast by inserting a sharp knife into the thickest side and cutting horizontally. Place the chicken breast between two pieces of waxed paper and gently pound until somewhat flattened. (Do not pound until thin, simply create a uniform thickness for even cooking.)

Pour the marinade over the breasts and allow them to

marinate 4 to 8 hours. Drain and pat the chicken dry when ready to stuff.

Spread 3/4 teaspoon of the mustard on each piece of ham. Place the cheese on the ham and fold the ham around the cheese. Place the ham and cheese into the pocket of the chicken.

Combine the flour, salt, pepper, paprika and cayenne. Immediately before cooking, dip each breast in the buttermilk, then dredge lightly in the seasoned flour. Refrigerate for 15 minutes.

Heat the butter in a heavy saute pan on medium until the foam subsides. Place the prepared breasts in the pan and brown lightly on each side. Lower the heat to medium-low and cook for approximately 4 minutes. Turn and continue cooking until done. Remove and place on a heated platter.

Pilsener Sauce:
A light, lovely sauce, this can also be served on fresh pasta that has been tossed with bits of leftover chicken, ham and fresh peas. Makes four half-cup servings.

        1 1/2 cups chicken broth
          1/2 cup German Pilsener
          1/2 teaspoon tarragon or thyme
            4 tablespoons pan drippings (add more butter if
                  needed)
            4 tablespoons flour

Combine the broth, beer and tarragon and heat until hot. Heat the drippings in the pan on medium heat. Sprinkle in the flour and cook, stirring constantly, for 4 minutes. Whisking continuously, slowly add the hot liquid and continue stirring until thickened. Serve over the sautéed breasts.

Stuffed Cornish Game Hens

These stuffed game hens were served as a stunning entree for the Conference Grand Banquet. The fine flavor of cave-aged Wisconsin blue cheese, in conjunction with citrus-edged Weissbier, rice, grapes and toasted walnuts, transforms these game hens into a memorable eating experience.

Stuffing:

1/2	cup basmati rice, washed thoroughly and soaked 8 to 12 hours
1/3	cup Weissbier
1 to 2	tablespoons olive oil
2	large shallots, thinly sliced
1/4	cup Italian parsley, finely chopped
1/2	cup Gorgonzola or 1/3 cup mild blue cheese, crumbled
1	cup very small, seedless green grapes
1/2	cup toasted walnuts, coarsely crushed
	pinch of fresh ground pepper

Combine the drained rice and beer in a small saucepan. Add 1 teaspoon olive oil and a pinch of salt. Bring to a simmer, cover and cook over low heat for 8 minutes. Remove from the heat and let sit, covered, for 10 minutes. Cool.

In a small skillet, saute the shallots in the remaining olive oil until soft and translucent. Cool. Combine the parsley, cheese, grapes and shallots. Toss in the cooled rice, toasted walnuts and pepper.

The Hens:

6	Rock Cornish game hens
1	fresh lemon, quartered

        1/2   pound butter, room temperature
          3   tablespoons fresh thyme, finely chopped
          4   large cloves garlic, finely minced and smashed
     1 1/2   cups Weissbier
              kosher salt and fresh ground pepper

Rinse and pat dry the game hens. Rub inside and out with the quartered lemon. Sprinkle the cavity lightly with the salt and pepper. In a small bowl, combine the butter, thyme and garlic, mashing well to incorporate thoroughly. Set aside.

Gently, without tearing, raise the skin from the breast on each of the game hens and push a bit of the herbed butter between the skin and the breast. Lightly stuff the body cavity of the game hens three-quarters full with the stuffing. Place a small piece of aluminum foil over the cavity entrance to keep the juices in and prevent the stuffing from falling out. Using cooking twine, truss the birds. Rub the hens well with some of the remaining herb butter. Salt and pepper lightly and place on a well-greased roasting rack, back side up.

Melt any remaining herb butter and add it to the beer for basting. Roast the hens at 400 degrees for 30 minutes. Baste and turn the hens breast side up. Continue roasting an additional 20 to 25 minutes, basting every 8 to 10 minutes. Check for doneness by moving a leg a bit to see if it moves freely, or check by puncturing the thickest part of the thigh meat to see if the juices run almost clear (beware of overcooking; the hens will become tough and tasteless).

The Sauce:
              Pan drippings with the fat removed (save 3 table-
                 spoons of fat)
          2   tablespoons blueberry, raspberry or Champagne
                 vinegar

1/4   cup Weissbier
  3   tablespoons honey
  1   shallot, finely minced
1/3   cup Italian parsley, finely chopped

Remove the cooked game hens and place on a warmed platter, covering them with foil to keep them hot. Pour the roasting drippings from the roaster into a gravy separator. Separate the pan juices from the drippings (fat). Pour the vinegar and beer over the pan and scrape pan to remove any browned bits and pieces left in the pan. Place these deglazed juices in a small saute pan along with the separated pan juices, 3 tablespoons of the drippings (optional), the honey and the shallot, and heat on medium-high. Reduce by one-third, add the parsley and pour over the game hens after serving.

MEAT

Cooking meat with beer is an old favorite of beer lovers around the world. Flemish beef stew (carbonnade), bigos (Polish hunters stew), etc., are but a few examples of this rich beer cooking heritage. Whether the meat is marinated in beer, basted with a beer-infused sauce, stewed or braised in beer, the result is always robust and satisfying.

Pork Speedies

Although Speedies are a culinary phenomenon of up-state New York (a favorite when ice-fishing) they deserve to be shared with the rest of the beer-loving community. Often made with lean pork, lamb or fresh game, Speedies are marinated in a spicy, herbed mixture before being skewered and grilled.

Marinade:
      1 cup Oktoberfest, smoked beer or Bavarian dark
    1/2 cup red wine vinegar
    1/2 cup olive oil
      1 teaspoon dried basil
      1 teaspoon dried parsley flakes
      2 teaspoons dried oregano
    1/4 teaspoon dried thyme
1/4 to 1/2 teaspoon hot pepper
           juice of 1/2 lemon
    1/2 small onion, very finely minced or grated
 4 to 8 cloves of garlic (to taste)
           salt and pepper, to taste
      4 pounds lean pork, cut into 1-inch cubes
           onions, peppers, small parboiled potatoes, apple
             chunks, etc.

Combine the marinade ingredients and pour over the pork chunks. Marinate at least 24 hours. Skewer the pork with the onions, peppers, potatoes and/or apples before grilling or broiling. Serve immediately.

Peppered Steak

The Midwest is home to corn-fed beef that literally melts in your mouth. Next time you crave a steak, treat yourself to corn-fed, U.S.D.A. Choice beef. For ease of preparation, try a boneless cut such as top sirloin, rib-eye or New York strip. Be sure to freshly crush your pepper for the fullest flavor!

      2 pounds (boneless weight) steaks, 1 to 1 1/2 inches
             thick
    1/2 cup strong ale or dark bock

4 large cloves of garlic, finely mashed
4 tablespoons black peppercorns, freshly crushed
1 tablespoon green peppercorns, freshly crushed
    (optional)
2 tablespoons canola oil mixed with 2 tablespoons
    olive oil
1 tablespoon kosher salt
4 tablespoons herbed butter

Combine the beer and garlic. Rub the mixture over the steak and let sit in the refrigerator for 1 hour. Pat the meat dry and press the crushed peppercorns into both sides. Let the steaks sit out at room temperature 30 to 40 minutes. Heat a serving platter and prepare a foil lid for it.

Heat a large, heavy-bottomed pan on medium-high until very hot. Pour in the oil and as soon as it is hot, sprinkle the kosher salt over the bottom and add the steaks (do not crowd them; cook two batches if necessary). Sear the meat for approximately 4 to 5 minutes on the first side or until the meat is a dark, crusty brown. Turn and continue to cook an additional 3 to 4 minutes, depending on how well done you prefer your steak.

Remove the meat from the pan and place it on the heated platter. Cover and allow it to sit for 5 minutes. Serve the hot steaks with 1 tablespoon of herbed butter on top of each.

Herbed Butter:
Please don't skip this extra. The flavorful "sauce" created when this mixes with the meat juices is superb.

1/4 pound unsalted butter, softened
2 teaspoons dried herbs or a herb mixture (thyme,
    basil, etc.)

1 shallot, finely minced
2 tablespoons lime juice

Beat the ingredients well, set aside.

Beerish Meatballs

These meatballs are blended with herbs and spices, browned and then simmered in a rich sauce of Oktoberfest beer, sour cream and onions. They are so tasty and easy to prepare, I chose them to serve during my lectures at the '92 Conference.

1/2 cup grated onion
2 tablespoons Oktoberfest beer
1/2 tablespoon salt
1 teaspoon thyme
2 teaspoons dried parsley
1 teaspoon freshly ground chili flakes
1 teaspoon cayenne pepper
1/2 teaspoon ground allspice
1/2 teaspoon fresh ground black pepper
1/2 teaspoon sugar
4 cloves garlic, finely minced and smashed
2/3 cup dried bread crumbs or 1 1/4 cups fresh bread
       crumbs
2 eggs
1/3 cup finely chopped parsley
2 pounds lean boneless beef or pork, freshly ground
    Olive oil for browning

Mix the first 11 ingredients together in a large bowl. Allow to steep for 15 minutes. Combine the remaining ingredients and the steeped spices, mixing thoroughly. Refrigerate 1 hour before forming into meatballs.

Heat a large, heavy skillet on medium heat. Add olive oil to just coat the bottom. Brown the meatballs on all sides. Layer the browned meatballs and onions in a large dutch oven. Pour the prepared sauce over the top. Cover and simmer slowly for 45 minutes. Serve hot.

Meatball Sauce:
     2 tablespoons vegetable oil
     4 cups sliced onions
   1/4 cup vegetable oil
   1/4 cup flour
 1 1/3 cups beef broth, hot
   2/3 cup Oktoberfest beer
     1 cup sour cream
     1 tablespoon paprika
   1/2 teaspoon cayenne (optional)
     2 cups sliced mushrooms (optional)
        salt and pepper to taste

Heat a large skillet or wok on medium-high heat. Swirl with the 2 tablespoons of oil and add the sliced onions. Stir-fry until golden and browned on the outside but still crisp. Set aside. Heat the oil and, when hot, sprinkle with the flour. Whisk thoroughly. Cook until a light golden brown in color. Whisk in the hot broth. When smooth, stir in the beer, sour cream, paprika, cayenne and mushrooms. Season to taste.

SEAFOOD

The delicate flavor of fresh seafood is a perfect match for the subtle innuendos of beer. Whether you marinate in beer, poach with beer, use beer sauces or steam in beer, your results will be excellent.

Remember not to overcook your fish. For juicy, exquisite fish, cook it 10 minutes per inch of thickness. Please refer to Schermerhorn (1991) for an in-depth discussion of cooking seafood.

Poached Fish with Herb Sauce

Any firm, white fish will work well with this dish. The poaching liquid and herbed sauce is fortified with the delicate, citrusy addition of Weissbier.

Poached Turbot:
       2 pounds of white fish fillets
       2 cups milk
1 1/2 cups Weissbier
1 1/2 cups chicken stock
       1 teaspoon *herbes fines*
       1 teaspoon salt

Combine the milk, beer, stock, herbs and salt. In a large, shallow pan (or poacher), bring the liquid to a medium simmer. Gently place the fish in the pan, cover and simmer, allowing 10 minutes cooking per inch of thickness. Remove the fillets gently, set aside on a warm dish and cover. Gently reduce the poaching liquid to 3 cups, being careful not to curdle it by overheating.

Herbed Weiss Sauce:
This is a rather decadent sauce, which is heavenly served over pasta or poached chicken, too.

    8 tablespoons butter
    8 tablespoons flour (all purpose)
    3 ounces Canadian bacon or quality ham, finely diced
    2 shallots, finely minced
    3 cups reduced poaching liquid (hot)
  1/2 cup Weissbier
  1/2 cup half-and-half or heavy cream
  1/2 cup Italian parsley, coarsely chopped
    2 tablespoons finely chopped fresh dill (or 2
         teaspoons dried)
       salt and pepper to taste

Melt the butter over medium-low heat until the foam subsides. Sprinkle in the flour, stirring briskly. Add the Canadian bacon and shallots, continuing to stir over medium-low heat. When the flour is well cooked (6 to 8 minutes) but not browned, slowly pour in the *hot* poaching liquid, whisking vigorously, until it is well incorporated.

Continue to simmer over medium-low heat until the sauce just begins to thicken. Combine the Weissbier and half-and-half. In a slow, steady stream, whisk in the beer and cream. Add 1/4 cup of the parsley and the dill. Cook over medium-low until the sauce thickens completely. Adjust seasonings with salt and pepper.

Arrange the fish on a platter. Ladle the sauce over the fillets, then sprinkle the remaining parsley over the top. Serve immediately.

Stuffed Shrimp

These opulent morsels of shrimp marinated with pale ale and stuffed with marinated cheese are a lovely appetizer. Better yet, serve them in great quantity for the main course!

        2 pounds uncooked jumbo shrimp (12 to 16 count),
              shelled
      1/2 cup olive oil
      1/2 cup pale ale
        1 tablespoon fresh lime or lemon juice
        4 large cloves garlic, mashed with 1/2 teaspoon salt
      1/4 cup finely chopped green onion
1/4 to 1/2 teaspoon fresh ground pepper
      1/2 cup quality olive oil
      1/4 cup balsamic vinegar
        2 tablespoons fresh lemon or lime juice
        4 cloves garlic, peeled and lightly mashed
    1 1/2 tablespoons fresh oregano or thyme, finely chopped
      1/4 teaspoon freshly ground pepper
  24 to 32 ounces Muenster cheese, finely cubed or coarsely
              grated
    1 1/2 cups fresh bread crumbs
          4-x-2-inch pieces of foil

Split the shrimp open along the back, cutting two-thirds
of the way through. Remove the vein and clean. Whisk the
next six ingredients together. Pour over the shrimp, tossing
gently. In a separate bowl, combine the remaining ingredients except for the bread crumbs.

Cover both the shrimp and the cheese mixtures and let
marinate in the refrigerator 2 to 6 hours. When ready to
assemble, stir the bread crumbs into the marinated cheese
mixture.

Place a shrimp, cut side up, on a piece of foil. Stuff with 2
to 3 tablespoons of the marinated cheese mixture. Wrap the
foil around the middle of the shrimp to keep the stuffing in
place. Grill or broil the shrimp over medium-high heat until
the shrimp just turn pink. Serve immediately.

VEGETABLES

There are many ways of adding beer to the cooking of vegetables. Whether used in the preparation of various soups or potato pancakes, beer in one form or another can add exquisite flavors to these treasures of the Midwest.

Minestrone

This classic Italian soup is rich with the garden-fresh vegetables that the Midwest is famous for growing. This soup was served as a first course at the Grand Banquet.

1/4 to 1/2 cup olive oil
    1 large onion, coarsely chopped
    4 ribs celery, coarsely chopped
    2 large carrots, coarsely chopped or sliced
    4 large cloves garlic, coarsely chopped and mashed
    2 teaspoons dried basil or 2 tablespoons fresh chopped basil
    1 teaspoon dried oregano or 1 tablespoon fresh chopped oregano
    3/4 cup Italian parsley, coarsely chopped (optional)
    8 cups rich stock, hot
1 1/2 cups American or German light lager beer
    3 cups cooked fava, great northern, marrow or navy beans
    4 medium white potatoes, scrubbed and cubed
    2 cups fresh snap beans, cleaned and snapped into 2-inch lengths
    2 cups zucchini, thickly sliced
    1 pound tomatoes, peeled and chopped (or canned if necessary)

salt and pepper to taste

1 cup tiny pasta—conchigliette, nochette or semini di melo

1 to 2 cups cabbage, thinly sliced

fresh grated Parmesan or homemade pesto for garnish

In a heavy kettle, heat the olive oil on medium heat. Add the onion, celery and carrots, sautéing until limp. Add the garlic, basil, oregano, and half the parsley, sautéing briefly until fragrant.

Stir in the stock, then add the beans and potatoes. Simmer slowly for 30 to 40 minutes or until the potatoes are tender. Add the snap beans, zucchini, tomatoes and seasonings. Simmer until tender.

Add the pasta and the remaining parsley and cabbage and continue simmering until the pasta is cooked. Serve with fresh grated cheese or a teaspoon of pesto floating on top.

Vegetarian Broth:

This makes an excellent vegetable-based broth for those who wish to make this a "vegetables only" soup.

2 large potatoes, cubed

1 onion, chopped

2 to 3 brown onion skins

1/2 cup barley

herbs such as bay leaves, thyme, basil, oregano, etc.

7 cups water

3 cups light bock beer

Any combination of the following: cabbage, celery ribs and tops, Italian parsley, garlic cloves, squash, peppercorns, salt, turnips, parsnips

Combine all ingredients in simmering water and cook until all flavor from the vegetables has been extracted. Strain and discard the vegetables. To make stock, reduce by one-half over medium-high heat.

Glazed Carrots and Parsnips

Richly glazed and colorful, this interesting medley of carrots and parsnips is elevated beyond the commonplace by the addition of brown ale.

    2 tablespoons butter
    1 tablespoon vegetable oil
    4 medium carrots, scrubbed and julienned
    4 medium parsnips, scrubbed, centers removed and
         julienned
    2 tablespoons sugar
    1 teaspoon powdered ginger (optional)
  1/3 cup brown ale or light bock
       fresh ground pepper to taste

Heat the butter and oil in a sauté pan on medium-low heat. Add the carrots and parsnips, tossing well with the butter. Sauté slowly for 15 minutes. Sprinkle the sugar, ginger and beer over the mixture and continue cooking slowly for 25 to 30 minutes, stirring occasionally. The vegetables should be lightly glazed, golden and limp when finished.

Potato Pancakes

These are a cross between hash-browns and traditional pancakes. Soaking the potatoes in Pilsener gives them a flavorful boost and adds to their crispness. Try them with a dollop of sour cream on top.

　4　large baking potatoes, peeled
　2　cups German Pilsener
　1　small onion, very finely minced
　1　teaspoon salt
1/2　teaspoon freshly ground pepper
　1　teaspoon paprika
　1　extra large egg
1/2　cup Italian flavored bread crumbs
1/4　cup grated hard cheese (Parmesan, Romano, etc.)
1/2 to 1　cup quality olive oil

Coarsely grate or finely julienne the potatoes. Place them in a bowl and pour the beer over the top. Cover and let sit for 1 hour. Drain the potatoes, reserving the beer for a stew. Stir the onion, salt, pepper, paprika, egg and bread crumbs in with the potatoes.

Heat a heavy skillet on medium until hot. Add just enough oil to lightly coat the bottom of the pan. Drop a few tablespoons of the potato mixture into the hot pan and flatten slightly. Sauté until crisp and golden brown (8 minutes), turn and brown the second side (5 minutes). If not serving immediately, place on a heated tray.

Hot Potato Salad

This is one of the finest potato salads to ever grace a table. The addition of Oktoberfest beer to the dressing breathes new life into this old-world dish.

　10　each—small new red and white potatoes, scrubbed
　6　strips lean bacon, coarsely chopped
　1　small onion, coarsely chopped
　2　shallots, coarsely chopped

5 scallions, cut diagonally into 1-inch pieces
2 teaspoons caraway seeds
1 cup Oktoberfest beer
4 tablespoons balsamic vinegar
6 tablespoons bacon drippings or olive oil
   Paprika, salt and pepper to taste
3 tablespoons toasted, crushed walnuts

Boil the potatoes in salted water until just tender (do not overcook). Drain the potatoes and cool slightly. Quarter the unpeeled potatoes.

In a heavy skillet, cook the bacon until crisp. Remove the bacon and set aside on towels to drain. Remove all but 6 tablespoons of the bacon drippings. Sauté the onion and shallot in the drippings until golden. Add the green onions and caraway seeds. Sauté for 1 minute. Add the beer to the onions and simmer over medium-high heat until reduced by half. Pour in the vinegar and drippings and simmer briefly. Adjust seasoning with salt and pepper.

Add the potatoes to the sauce and simmer for 2 minutes, turning gently. Remove from the heat and place in a bowl. Sprinkle with the crumbled bacon, paprika and walnuts.

DESSERTS

Using beer in preparing desserts is akin to Columbus locating the New World. A boundless area of exploration and discovery lies ahead, filled with possibilities and surprises. Trust me—the alliance of toasty stout and chocolate in truffles, or of rich, golden Altbier with an elegant bread pudding will convince even the most doubting that cooking desserts with beer merits further investigation.

Stout-and-Bourbon Truffles

Truffles are candies made from melted chocolate and cream, chilled and formed into roughly shaped balls before being rolled in unsweetened cocoa powder. A beer lovers' chocolate dream come true, these are intensified with the addition of stout and whiskey.

        8 ounces of fine, extra dark chocolate, chopped finely
      1/3 cup stout
        3 tablespoons heavy cream
        4 tablespoons sweet butter
1/2 to 2/3 cup powdered sugar
        2 tablespoons quality whiskey
      1/2 cup pecans, toasted at 350 degrees 12 minutes, then
             chopped

Heat the stout, heavy cream and butter until bubbles form around the edges of the pan. Remove from the heat and add the chocolate, stirring constantly until the chocolate is completely melted and the mixture is smooth. Stir in the whiskey and nuts.

Refrigerate until firm, 2 to 4 hours. Use a melon baller or a small scoop to form the mixture into small, rough shaped balls. Roll in Dutch-process cocoa powder, toasted nuts, lightly toasted coconut or finely crushed pralines, or dip in additional melted chocolate.

Beer-Laced Carrot Cakes

These miniature cakes are perfect for parties and picnics. Not overly sweet, they are packed with coconut, pecans and pineapple in a light bock batter. The citrus and bock glaze complements the rich, moist texture of the cakes.

   1 cup shredded coconut (toasted at 350 degrees for 12 minutes)
   1 cup walnuts or pecans (toasted at 350 degrees for 12 minutes)
   1 pound carrots, peeled
   2 cups granulated sugar
   2 cups unbleached flour
 1/2 teaspoon salt
 1/2 tablespoon cinnamon
 1/2 teaspoon allspice
 1/4 teaspoon freshly grated nutmeg
   2 teaspoons baking soda
   8 tablespoons cold butter, cut into small pieces
 1/2 cup vegetable oil
 1/2 cup light bock
   4 large eggs
   2 teaspoons grated orange rind
   2 teaspoons vanilla
 2/3 cup crushed pineapple, drained and patted dry

Grease and flour 36 petite tart pans and place on a large baking sheet or pan.

Place the carrots in a food processor and process until finely chopped, or grate them on a grater. Combine the carrots, sugar, flour, salt, cinnamon, allspice, nutmeg, soda and butter in a bowl and mix well.

Combine the oil, beer, eggs, orange rind and vanilla in a separate bowl. Pour the liquid ingredients over the dry ingredients and beat well. Fold in the coconut, nuts and pineapple, stirring well.

Fill the tart pans two-thirds full. Bake in a 350-degree oven for 15 to 17 minutes or until a pale gold. To check, insert a toothpick into the center of one. Remove from the oven and cool for 10 minutes. Invert the pans over your hand to remove. If the cake sticks a bit, use a toothpick to help loosen it.

Place the cakes bottom-side up on a cooling rack over a shallow pan. Pour the prepared glaze (recipe follows) over the tops and allow to set 5 minutes before transferring to a platter. Garnish with strips of decorative orange zest, candied violets, etc.

Orange Glaze:

    3 cups powdered sugar
    3 tablespoons orange juice concentrate, undiluted
2 to 3 tablespoons bock
    4 tablespoons heavy cream

Combine all the ingredients and stir until well mixed. You may need to heat the glaze slightly when pouring it over the cakes. To heat, place the bowl over a pan of simmering water for a few minutes.

Bread Pudding

Bread pudding is the ultimate in simple comfort food. This recipe goes well beyond the basics by adding the richness of Altbier, baking it in a handsome kugelhopf mold and serving it with a luscious beer and caramel sauce.

     10 large eggs, separated
      1 cup brown sugar, firmly packed
 5 to 6 cups half-and-half (less cream equals firmer texture)
      2 cups Altbier

      1/4   cup creme de cacao
        2   tablespoons orange zest, finely chopped
        8   cups Italian or French bread, torn in small chunks
        1   cup raisins soaked in liqueur of your choice
        2   apples, peeled, cored and chopped (optional)
      2/3   cup toasted nuts, coarsely chopped (optional)
        1   cup toasted coconut (optional)
        1   large buttered kugelhopf pan
 3/4 to 1   cup white sugar

Beat the egg yolks until light and fluffy. Beat in the brown sugar. Stir in the half-and-half, beer, creme de cacao and orange zest. Set aside.

Combine the torn bread, raisins, apples, nuts and coconut. Pour in the yolk mixture and coat the bread thoroughly.

In a large bowl, whip the egg whites until frothy. Add the white sugar and continue whipping until stiff peaks form. Gently fold the egg whites into the bread mixture until well combined.

Carefully spoon the mixture into the buttered pan. Place the pan in a larger pan of water and bake at 325 degrees for 1 1/2 hours or until a knife inserted into the middle comes out clean. Cool 30 minutes. Run a thin-bladed knife around the center tube of the mold, releasing the pudding. Gently shake and twist the mold until the remainder of the pudding releases from the sides. Turn out onto a platter. Serve with beer-and-caramel sauce (see recipe on page 57).

MISCELLANEOUS CONDIMENTS AND SAUCES

From mustard to caramel sauce, here are some of the best "little" recipes available.

Sweet-and-Hot Beer Mustard

Although this was included in *Brew Free or Die* and also appeared in the very first "Brewgal Gourmet" article in *zymurgy* (Vol. 14, No. 1), it must be included here, just in case you missed it.

        1/4 cup dry mustard powder
        1/3 cup light or dark bock, Oktoberfest, or Altbier
          2 tablespoons rice vinegar
scant 1/4 cup sugar
          1 tablespoon prepared horseradish
        1/2 teaspoon dried tarragon or thyme
          2 egg yolks, beaten

Whisk together all but the egg yolks. Cover and let sit 30 minutes. Whisk in the yolks and place over a double boiler. Cook on medium-low until thickened, whisking constantly. Cool. This will keep for up to 3 weeks in the refrigerator.

Variations:
Curry Mustard: In place of the 1 tablespoon of horseradish, use 1/2 tablespoon horseradish plus 2 level teaspoons of curry powder (or to taste).
Honey Mustard: Use 1/2 cup honey instead of sugar and use 3 egg yolks instead of 2 yolks.
Herbed Mustard: Add 1 tablespoon of your favorite fresh herb (finely chopped) such as basil, thyme, tarragon, etc.

Sweet Beer Sauce

This amalgam of rich beer, sugar, butter and eggs is phenomenal on the Belgian waffles.

    1/2 stick butter
      2 cups sugar
      2 eggs
    3/4 cup dark bock or porter
      1 teaspoon vanilla

Melt butter in a large sauce pan. In a medium bowl, beat eggs into the sugar until well blended and fluffy. Slowly add the beer, whisking thoroughly. Add the beer mixture to the butter and stir. Slowly bring to a full, rolling boil. Boil over medium heat 6 to 8 minutes without stirring. Remove from heat and stir in the vanilla. Strain, cool and store in the refrigerator.

Beer-and-Caramel Sauce

This velvety beer-and-caramel sauce is the ultimate in caramel flavor, enhanced by the distinctive richness of ale. Try it on sundaes or with the elegant Bread Pudding.

    1/2 cup unsalted butter
    1/3 cup Lyles Golden Syrup or corn syrup
      1 cup raw sugar, ground finely in a blender
    1/2 cup brown ale or India pale ale
    1/2 cup heavy cream

Warm the butter and syrup on medium-low. Add the sugar and stir until dissolved. Add the beer and cream. Bring to a low boil and cook without stirring for 6 minutes. Cool.

Keep this refrigerated. Warm gently on the stove or in a microwave, stirring well before each use.

Candy Schermerhorn lives in Phoenix, Arizona, and is a culinary consultant and instructor at Kitchen Classics. She takes great joy in educating the public about beer and its culinary potential through her cooking classes. This enthusiasm for homebrew cooking has prompted her to begin writing a full-length cookbook devoted to the art and joy of cooking with beer, to be published in 1993 by Brewers Publications.

REFERENCES

Schermerhorn, C. (1991). The Brewgal Gourmet cooks with beer. In *Brew Free or Die* (pp. 179-205). Boulder, Colo.: Brewers Publications.

5. Improving Extract Beers

Ron Downer
Owner, The Brewhaus homebrew supply store

Most beginners start with extract beers and, therefore, have their initial problems with them. As newcomers become more experienced, they usually either learn what is needed to improve their beers, or they give up and quit the hobby, an occurrence that was all too common just a few years ago when bad advice and substandard ingredients were prevalent. This paper addresses several relatively simple ways in which beginning homebrewers can improve their extract brews.

PREPARING THE WORT

The proliferation of one-can kits in the homebrew market has made it so simple to brew a 5-gallon batch of beer that many beginning brewers make the mistake of not delving into

Ron Downer

the ample literature on brewing that is available, relying instead on the printed instructions on the can of extract. Unfortunately, the large majority of one-can kits on the market today instruct the user how to make beer quickly and cheaply, not how to make it the best it can be. My first bit of advice for improving beers—and in this case I mean specifically beers made from one-can kits—is to disregard the instructions on the can until malt extract manufacturers become as enlightened as American homebrewers.

Malt vs. Sugar

The biggest mistake homebrewers made just a few years ago was to use sugar as a major ingredient in their beers. Many beginners still have the mistaken notion that sugar, specifically corn or cane sugar, is a necessary component of beer. Nothing could be further from the truth. Sugar does increase the alcoholic strength of the beer, but it does so at the expense of malt flavor, which is supposed to be the dominant flavor in good beers. The sweetness in beers that some beginners believe is produced by adding sugar is actually contributed by malt. One of the biggest complaints I hear about homebrew is that it tastes cidery or winy. These tastes are caused, in most instances, by the addition of too much refined sugar. My advice is to make all-malt beers, by replacing the sugar called for in many recipes, and on most one-can kits, with either an equal amount of dry malt extract or with a second can of malt extract for each 5- to 6-gallon batch of beer. Sugar and dry malt are not exactly interchangeable on a one-to-one basis, but for our purposes, equal amounts of dry malt extract can be used as a substitute for sugar with good results. It costs a little more to make all-malt beers, but the improvement in taste is well worth the added expense. If you feel you must add sugar to cut costs try to keep the proportions down to 75 percent malt, 25 percent sugar. Five cups of corn sugar is sufficient for a 4-pound one-can kit. Don't be overly concerned about the alcoholic strength of your beer, as the malt extract will provide the required level of alcohol while also giving more taste and character to your beer.

Boiling the Wort

A fairly disturbing addition to some beer kit labels is the phrase, "No boiling required." This bit of advice can only lead to substandard or even ruined beers. Boiling the wort is a necessary step that has several purposes:
1. Clarification of the wort.
2. Extraction of hop bitterness and flavor when unhopped extracts are used.
3. Sterilization of the wort.
4. Reduction in the volume of the wort.

Wort that has never been boiled will contain undesirable levels of proteins, which can cause hazy beer that is especially prone to oxidation and spoilage. We can never know for sure whether a wort was boiled prior to being reduced to syrup form, so a rolling boil for 15 to 30 minutes is necessary to help precipitate excess proteins out of solution. It will give an indication of whether or not the wort was actually boiled by the extract manufacturer. The point at which the proteins coagulate into large flakes that can easily be seen settling out of a sample of the wort is called the hot break. A rolling boil, not a simmer, is required to coagulate the proteins into large flakes, because this is not just a chemical process but also a physical one that involves collisions of the smaller flakes during the boil. Exposing wort to a good rolling boil until the hot break occurs will greatly enhance the clarity of your finished beer and will also help prolong the storage life, which commercial brewers refer to as the shelf life.

When using unhopped extracts it is necessary to add hops. They must be boiled in the wort to extract their bitterness, which is required to balance the sweetness of the malt and to infuse the beer with the preservative properties of the hop plant. Hopped extracts will not, of course, require a boil for extracting bitterness from hops, but they will need boiling to sterilize the wort and to utilize what are referred to as finishing hops. You may have noticed that beers made from only hopped extract, with no hops added by the brewer, lack a good hop character. Unless you are brewing a very heavy beer characterized mainly by its malty aroma you will probably want to add some finishing or aroma hops near the end of the boil. They give the beer a nice hop aroma and additional hop flavor without adding more bitterness. If you have already fermented your beer and discover a glaring lack of hop character you can add two or three drops of hop oil per 12 ounces of beer just prior to bottling or kegging. The addition of some bittering hops is usually necessary when using unhopped dry malt extract as a replacement for sugar in a recipe—while sugar completely ferments, the malt does not, and so requires some hop bitterness to balance its sweetness.

A boil of not less than 30 minutes should be used with pelletized hops, and whole leaf hops require a boil of an hour or more. A finished beer that is obviously lacking in sufficient bitterness can be salvaged by using a commercially prepared hop extract such as isomerized hop extract, which, unlike hop oil, provides bitterness rather than aroma and flavor.

Sterilizing the wort is of utmost importance in producing high quality beer. Giving a high priority to sterilizing the fermentation, racking and bottling equipment only to put unsterilized wort into it seems like an futile exercise, but that is exactly what many brewers do when they fail to boil the wort. The malt extract in a kit may have been pasteurized, but all dry ingredients, such as dry malt or corn sugar, have not been through a sterilization process. They must be boiled with the wort in order to kill any bacterias, molds or wild yeasts that might be lurking in them and that could spoil the beer's taste or appearance. Unless you are very sure about your cold topping-up water it is a good idea to boil it, too. Cool overnight in a closed container before pouring it into your fermenter.

Extract brewers will not usually find it necessary to use the boil to reduce the volume of the wort, unless they have added excessive water.

Specialty Grains

Using specialty grains with extract is a widely used method of improving beer quality without moving into the realm of all-grain brewing. Partial mashes are sometimes recommended as a method of improving extract beers, but unless you do not have the facilities to conduct a full mash I think it is largely a waste of time. A partial mash takes just as much time and energy to perform as a full scale mash does. The best alternative is to use a portion of specialty grains to add character to your extract beer. Grains such as crystal malt, chocolate malt, black malt and roasted barley do not require mashing to extract their goodness. Just crack the grains, place them into a pot with 2 or more quarts of cold water and bring to a boil. As soon as the boil commences, cut the heat off and strain the grains from the liquid. Add the liquid to your wort before boiling and discard the spent grains. Regardless of what some recipes may say, do not boil the grains, because prolonged boiling will extract undesirable tannins that will cause your beer to be astringent. You can recognize astringency in a beer as that dry, puckering sensation in your mouth. Crystal malt is the most widely used specialty grain because it confers more than one benefit on beer—it improves head retention, adds a caramel-like sweetness, and adjusts the color from a slightly reddish tinge to a deeper reddish-brown hue.

AFTER THE BOIL

Thus far I have mainly discussed procedures and ingredients that are used during the preparation of the wort. Now it is time to consider what can be done at the later stages of the brewing process to improve the final product.

Cooling the Boiled Wort

When boiled wort is chilled rapidly, such as in a counterflow wort chiller, it undergoes a process called a cold break. During the cold break additional protein precipitates from the wort in a more powdery form than the larger flakes obtained during the hot break. If the cooled wort is then siphoned off this additional protein sediment, fermentation will be much cleaner and less of the hop bittering substances will be lost in the "trub." Grain brewers use some sort of wort chiller to cool their wort quickly, but for extract brewers rapid chilling of the wort can be a major problem, even when cold water has been used to top up the hot wort in the fermenter. During slow cooling the brewer does not get a cold break, and the wort is left open to possible contamination during the time it takes to cool down to yeast pitching temperature. I am not suggesting that extract brewers invest in a brew chiller, although it is a very good idea, but leaving the wort to cool overnight is generally asking for trouble. The only alternative to using a brew chiller is to place the covered boiling pot of hot wort in a sink full of cold water, or in an ice bath, for 15 to 30 minutes before adding it to the fermenter. Then use sterile, refrigerated water to top the fermenter up to the proper level. Whatever method you decide to use, try to cool the wort to yeast pitching temperature as rapidly as possible.

Yeast Starters

I consider yeast to be the single most important ingredient in brewing. Without good yeast you may as well resign yourself to producing mediocre or even undrinkable beers. It is amazing how many brewers will purchase the best malts and finest hops for their beers and then buy the cheapest yeast they can find to add to these quality ingredients. If you can afford the best ingredients for your beers you should be either culturing pure yeast cultures or buying the more expensive, cleaner dry yeasts (use a 12- or 14-gram packet, or two of the smaller size packets, for each 5-gallon batch). If you need more motivation for purchasing the better yeasts let me quote from a recent article published by a major yeast manufacturer: "Why should many kits come with plain baker's yeast despite what is said on the sachet?" Following this question the article says, "The British kit manufacturers have become accustomed to buying yeast as cheap as it can possibly be.

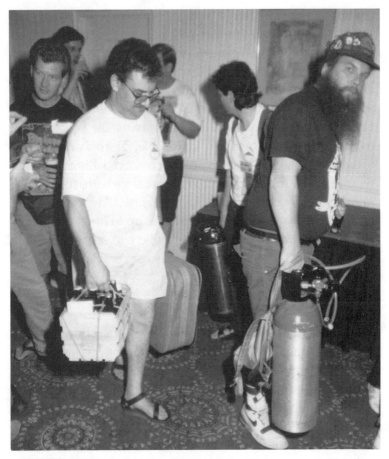

Conference attendees arrived in Milwaukee well supplied with homebrew to share.

Quality, in professional yeast terms, costs money and many kit manufacturers are not willing to pay the extra to enhance their product." If that statement doesn't prompt a lot of homebrewers to upgrade their yeast, nothing will.

The new pure culture yeasts, packed in what I call a bag kit, are simple to use and are very inexpensive if you consider the alternative of losing an entire batch of beer to contaminated yeast. All pure cultures and most dry yeasts are best used in an active starter to reduce the lag time between pitching the yeast and the onset of fermentation. A starter also gives you a chance to evaluate the yeast prior to pitching it. If the starter does not taste or smell right, there is a very good possibility that your finished beer won't, either. Throw it out if there is a bad taste or odor in it. For a more complete discussion of preparing and using yeast starters I recommend reading *Yeast Culturing for the Homebrewer* (Leistad, 1983) and the 1989 Special Yeast Issue of *zymurgy* magazine. If you are brewing on impulse and do not have a yeast starter ready to go, you can still reduce lag time by adding the dry yeast to one-half cup of 104 degree F (40 degree C) water 15 minutes prior to yeast pitching time. This procedure will rapidly rehydrate the yeast under favorable conditions and "wake it up" from hibernation. Yeast that lies under the warm water without showing any signs of activity should be discarded, because it is probably not viable.

Sanitation

If all homebrewers paid as much attention to sanitation as commercial brewers do we could skip this subject, but even the best homebrewers eventually become lax in their sanitizing procedures and experience contamination problems as a result. Beer, unlike wine, has neither the alcohol content nor the very low pH that inhibits the growth of unwanted organisms. Beer will not harbor pathogenic organisms that could be fatal, but it can provide a fertile growth medium for a lot of contaminants that will make your beer unpalatable. Therefore, everything that touches your beer, whether in the cooled wort stage or the packaging process, must be clean and well sanitized. It really doesn't matter whether you use a commercially prepared sterilant such as Chempro SDP, B-Brite, and Iodophor or a solution of generic household bleach, just as long as you use something. Soak all equipment, including fermenters, plastic spoons, test equipment, bottles, etc., for a minimum of 30 minutes and then rinse with very hot water to remove all traces of the sterilant. Do this religiously until it becomes an ingrained habit and you will never experience the agony of defeat by spoilage organisms and wild yeasts.

Fermentation Temperatures

Although fermenting within the proper temperature range may seem elementary to experienced brewers, this concept is widely misunderstood or not even conceived of by many beginners. Both ale and lager yeasts can sucessfully be used in the temperature range of 55 to 65 degrees F (13 to 18 degrees C), but optimum results are obtained by fermenting with the ale yeast at 60 to 70 degrees F (15.5 to 21 degrees C) and with the lager yeast at 50 to 60 degrees F (10 to 15.5 degrees C), although lager yeast will tolerate even lower temperatures. Fermenting too warm for the chosen strain of yeast will cause it to produce a host of off-flavors which can range from barely drinkable to completely intolerable. If you have no other choice, due to a lack of adequate temperature control facilities, try to keep all ferments at room temperature, which is normally 70 to 75 degrees F (15.5 to 24 degrees C).

Single-stage Fermentation

When I speak of single-stage fermentation as a means of improving beer I mean bypassing the plastic fermenter stage and fermenting completely in glass or metal containers using the blowoff method. This method of fermentation will usually produce superior beers if the majority of protein trub is removed before fermentation starts. The single-stage blowoff method does not produce better beer because of anything that is blown out of the overflow tube but because the beer is not opened to possible contamination or oxidation during the racking from primary to secondary fermenter. The use of a blowoff tube has received a lot of negative publicity from a small segment of homebrewers who had bad experiences with this system, caused by the use of improper equipment. *The New Complete Joy of Home Brewing* (Papazian, 1991), for instance, contains an illustration showing a length of small diameter tubing being used as a blowoff tube. When such a small diameter tube becomes plugged with trub or hop residue enough pressure builds inside the carboy to cause a dangerous explosion of flying glass. I recommend using tubing with an inside diameter of one inch for blowoff tube. This tubing will fit snugly in the neck of most carboys without a drilled stopper, and nothing that foams out of the beer will clog it up. There is absolutely no reason not to improve your fermentation by using the blowoff system as long as you use proper equipment and common sense.

Additives

We have already spoken about adding specialty grains to improve your beer in the brewing stage, but there are other additives that can be used to improve the beer just prior to bottling or kegging. Malto-dextrin is a white powder that can be added to provide additional body and mouthfeel to a beer that would otherwise taste too thin. Eight ounces or more of malto-dextrin may be boiled in water and added to 5 gallons of beer without affecting its taste or color.

Clarifiers will not necessarily improve the taste of your

beer but they will improve its appearance and the perception of taste. Most beer drinkers will think that a clear beer tastes better than a cloudy beer, whether it does or not. Beginning homebrewers often take instructions quite literally. When the instructions say that the beer will be finished fermenting in one week they don't think about it being too cloudy for bottling, so they bottle too soon and get excessive sediment. Beer finings, particularly isinglass finings, will help impatient brewers clear suspended yeast from their finished beer in record time. Isinglass is now readily available in both liquid and easy-to-use powder form. Traditional gelatin finings are a lower priced alternative to isinglass, but they do not seem to work as well or as fast. A beer that appears clear when warm may develop a haze when it is chilled, because the proteins causing the haze come out of solution.

The best method of removing chill haze, if you have a spare refrigerator, is to chill the beer as cold as possible and leave it long enough for the chill haze proteins to settle out. Siphon the cleared beer into another container while it is still cold and you will leave the troublesome proteins behind in the sediment. The only other alternative is to use polyclar, a powdered plastic polymer that is used in the brewing industry to remove chill haze proteins from beer before it is filtered. Use one-quarter cup of polyclar per 5 gallons of beer. The cleared beer must be very carefully siphoned off the sediment to keep from disturbing the polyclar, which can be easily picked up and transferred during the racking procedure. A rough filtration, for those who have the equipment, will remove any polyclar left in the beer.

Whatever the problems with your extract beer, whether they be actual or potential, there is a procedure or additive that can assist you in solving them. You are not stuck with what you get in a can of malt extract as long as you realize that an extensive list of options is available for improving your extract beer.

> *Ron Downer has a B.S. in education from the University of Tennessee. He has been involved with homebrewing for more than 20 years and is the owner of The Brewhaus, a national mail-order retailer/wholesaler of home beer- and wine-making supplies. Ron is also Brewmaster of the newly-formed Smoky Mountain Brewing Company, a microbrewery that will open in east Tennessee in 1993.*

REFERENCES AND SUGGESTED READING

Leistad, R. (1983). *Yeast Culturing for the Homebrewer*. Ann Arbor, Mich.: G. W. Kent, Inc.

Papazian, C. (1991). *The New Complete Joy of Home Brewing*. New York: Avon Books.

Yeast and Beer (1989). [Special Issue] *zymurgy*. 12:4.

6. Recipe Formulation

Doug Henderson
Author, The Recipe Formulator

It is difficult to address a topic as large as recipe formulation without also considering another topic that goes hand in hand with it—namely, beer style variation. What makes an English bitter so rich and full in flavor with so little malt? Why does a Russian imperial stout or a bock leave one with a slightly hot flavor on the tongue? These questions bring to mind the excitement and challenge of understanding what makes different beers so . . . different. To address these concerns, we will take a quick tour through a list of ingredients, discussing how they relate to beer style variations, and then walk through a few recipe formulations. You may find that a lot is left unsaid, but please don't despair. There are excellent sources for reading further about style variation and recipe formulation, and I have tried to reference as many as possible. What I hope to do here is provide enough background information to make you excited to learn more. May we all brew better beers for it.

Doug Henderson

To better understand beer style variations and recipe formulation, we can start by examining the ingredients that typically go into making traditional beers.

INGREDIENTS

The main components of beer can be loosely defined as water, malted barley, malted wheat, hops and yeast. Adjuncts also need to be mentioned since they are an integral part of some beer styles. An adjunct, in my opinion, is anything other than the five ingredients listed above. The Reinheitsgebot (the Bavarian purity law of 1516) actually states that only water, malted barley, malted wheat and hops may be used to make beer. The gap between my list and that specified in the Reinheitsgebot is due to the fact that yeast was not discovered until 1680, and was not isolated and controlled until 1867, by Louis Pasteur. We will cover the ways in which water, malted barley, hops and yeast are combined to help determine a particular beer style.

Water

From the lime well sunk over 200 years ago in Tadcaster, England, to the water from Burton on the river Trent, to the aqueous sources in Dublin, Ireland, there are many different types of water that help characterize certain world styles of beer. Water is the ingredient that accounts for between 80 and

95 percent of the volume of any beer and is an essential one to understand to better emulate classic beer styles. Let us focus briefly on water composition and how it relates to stylistic variations.

Our water supplies usually originate from rain. As this rain passes through various geologic formations, it acquires certain attributes from the mineral salts it absorbs. The level and kind of minerals the water acquires can be thought of as the natural starting point for brewers of the past, who didn't necessarily know (or weren't able to change) the water they brewed with.

Let's look at Table 1 to get an idea of the differences between some famous waters. It lists the distinct ions that are present (in parts per million) in areas that are celebrated for specific beer styles.

TABLE 1
Famous Water

	Burton	Dortmund	Dublin	Munich	Pilsen	Vienna
Calcium	300	225	117	75	7	200
Carbonate	0	180	0	150	15	120
Chloride	26	60	19	2	5	12
Magnesium	42	40	4	18	2	60
Sodium	54	60	12	2	2	8
Sulfate	720	120	54	10	5	125

Ions that play a significant role in the brewing process include the following: calcium (Ca), magnesium (Mg), carbonate (HCO_3), sulfate (SO_4) and chlorine (Cl). The presence of these ions in various concentrations will contribute certain flavors to your beer. Sometimes they interact with other minerals and ions, sometimes with other ingredients like hops.

For instance, calcium helps acidify the mash, and magnesium helps proper yeast development in the brewing process. We will be focusing on the roles of various substances in the brewing process, so we will stop here without a complete technical exposure to the chemistry of brewing water and instead defer to George Fix (1989). He has a wonderful description of water chemistry and the effects of brewing salts starting on page 7 of his *Principles of Brewing Science*.

As an example of the relevance of water to recipe formulation, let's look at what Darryl Richman (1989) has to say about the water in Munich, Germany:

> First of all, just looking at the numbers explains a lot about the kinds of beers produced in the Munich area. Their beers are colorful— from the Bocks and Doppelbocks through Märzens, and Dunkels to the Dunkel Weizens, they are all darker beers. Perhaps this stems from that fact that, to obtain the proper level of acidity, more dark malt is needed to balance out the carbonate water (p. 32).

He goes on to explain that since a good mash needs a slightly acidic environment (pH approximately 5.3), the calcium level from the salt calcium carbonate needs to be high enough to help form a slightly acidic environment. "Dark malts come to the rescue because they add their own acidity and stabilize this tendency toward alkalinity" (p. 32). The water in the Munich area, high in both calcium and carbonate, is ideally suited for producing darker beer styles.

Let's look at another example. In Table 1 we see that Burton has a rather high calcium sulfate (gypsum) level. This area is renowned for its pale ales. Worthington White Shield is a good example of a classic pale ale from Burton. I've noticed that some of the bitters brewed in the United Kingdom have a slightly sulfurous note to them, which makes sense since there is a high level of sulfate coming from the local water supplies. We can also see from the table that the water in that area is quite high in calcium. Since we learned from our previous example that we need to have a slightly acidic pH for our water, we should examine the interaction of the ions for a pale ale. Terry Foster (1990) explains this well:

> In dark beers, the roasted malts used are high enough in acidity to override the effects of bicarbonate. In pale ales there is not enough acidity in the grist to do this, and the pH depends entirely on the ionic content of the water. . . . Certain ions also affect beer flavor, their effect being more pronounced in pale than in dark beers. Sulphate is very important in this respect, imparting a dryness to the beer which accentuates the hop bitterness in a pale ale. . . . Burton water also contains sodium and chloride ions. These contribute both fullness and mouth feel to the beer, which helps add some complexity in the case of pale ales, although their effect is reduced by the presence of high level of sulphates (pp. 58-59).

From these two examples we have seen that water does have quite an effect on certain beer styles. This means that simulating the water used to brew a certain world beer style can help us target that style more effectively. Although it is beyond the scope of this paper to go into too much detail about water treatment, many good articles have been written on the subject. I found the discussions in Richman (1989), Miller (1988), Line (1985), Noonan (1986), and Briggs, Hough, Stevens and Young (1981) to be quite useful. Later we will look at how I have dealt with water treatment in my Hyper-Card brewing stack called the Recipe Formulator.

Malted Barley

Malted barley is another essential ingredient in the composition of beer. We focus here on two significant contributions malt makes to beer styles—flavor and color. To better understand how malt helps produce style variations let's examine some recipes for several different styles (see Table 2).

TABLE 2
Malt in Style

	AHA STYLE	SUBCATEGORY	MALT (% OF TOTAL)						
			Pale	Lager	Vienna	Black Patent	Dextrine	Wheat	Crystal
1.	American Light Lager	b. American Standard		77					
2.	Classic Pilsener	a. Bohemian		84	5		11		
3.	English & Scottish Bitter	a. English Ordinary	92						8
4.	English & Scottish Bitter	c. English Special	91					3.5	5.5
5.	Stout	a. Classic Dry Stout		73					
6.	Stout	d. Imperial Stout	80			3.3		3.3	
7.	Wheat Beer	d. German-style Weizen		33				67	

Adjuncts are present in:
1. 23 percent flaked maize
5. 13.3 percent flaked barley, 13.3 percent roast barley
6. 16.7 percent dark brown sugar

Recipe Sources:
1. Miller, 1988, p. 201.
2. Miller, 1990, derived from reading text.
3. Foster, 1990, p. 113.
4. Foster, 1990, p. 114.
5. Miller, 1988, p. 230.
6. Miller, 1988, p. 233.
7. Miller, 1988, p. 217.

All the recipes I have chosen are from accomplished brewers, and I believe they reflect the styles well.

A quick glance at the table shows us that pale malt is the major component of all these styles, with the noted exception of the Weizen (wheat beer) recipe, which uses about two-thirds wheat malt and one-third pale ale malt. As we examine the chart a little more closely we can see a broad distinction between lagers and ales, with the primary differences in malt types being between pale lager malt and pale ale malt.* Since pale malts make the most significant contribution to most of these styles, let's look for a minute at the difference between pale lager and ale malts. Much of the following discussion is paraphrased from the Pale Malts chapter in *The Complete Handbook of Home Brewing* (Miller, 1988).

In general, pale lager malts have thinner husks than pale ale malts and, thus, have a lower polyphenol content. Lager malts are used in many super-premium American lagers and are the only type of malt used in Germany. In addition, the two-row lager malts (when being malted) are kilned at low temperatures. This helps preserve the lighter color that results from using this malt. Pale lagers may have a substantial quantity of DMS (dimethyl sulfide) present. DMS gives off a sweet corn aroma to a lager mash, and when fermented can add a pleasant malty quality to the finished product. This aroma is acceptable in small quantities for a lager. Although I may draw heat from the extract brewers in the crowd, I'll say that it is fairly difficult to get the color right when brewing a lager beer from extract. The act of manufacturing extract caramelizes it, which can make it difficult to get the very light straw-colored tone that is appropriate for a pale bock or an American light lager. More likely a darker golden color will

---

* Of course, there are exceptions. See Miller (1988), pp. 227-230.

result from using extract. This is acceptable for a pale ale, which typically runs towards a golden and perhaps even an amber color. Color, with respect to style, will be discussed under specialty malts.

Pale ale malts are fully modified and undergo a long kilning process. Miller (1988) says:

> Another result of the long kilning is that ale malt has very little s-methyl methionine (SMM) and dimethyl sulfoxide (DMSO)—two chemical compounds which, when heated, are converted into *dimethyl sulfide* (DMS). This is the stuff which gives that sweet creamed corn aroma to a lager mash. Many pale lagers have perceptible amounts of DMS, but it is never noticeable in British ale. This is one reason to reserve each type of malt for the styles of beer which are traditionally made from it (p. 49).

Pale lager malt is appropriate for your lager creations, and pale ale malt—whether you choose British or domestic—should be employed in the creation of ales. Byron Burch tells us in *Brewing Quality Beers* that "British pale malt will be a bit darker, tending to give your beer a gold color. It also has a somewhat different flavor than the American" (Burch, 1990, p. 24).

Specialty Malts

One way you can greatly affect beer style is by the proper use of specialty malts. These include Munich, Vienna, crystal, black patent, chocolate, dextrine and wheat malts. Munich and Vienna malts are lightly toasted malts that contribute an amber color, some body and a malty sweetness. Wheat malt can give a lighter, cleaner taste than equivalent quantities of barley, and provides a good way of getting a better head on your beer. Crystal malt (depending on the color) can give both a darker color and a sweetness to your beer. It will also help with head retention. Black patent malt imparts mainly color to your beer, but if used in sufficient quantity will produce a dry, burnt flavor. Chocolate malt contributes a nutty or toasted flavor. Dextrine malt is used almost exclusively to give more body to your beer. It does not have any enzymes, so brewers must rely on the enzymes in other malts when mashing with it. These are, of course, rough sketches of the characteristics these particular specialty malts add to your beer. For more information, I refer you to a few good sources: *The New Complete Joy of Home Brewing*, pp. 51–59 (Papazian, 1991); *Brewing Quality Beers*, pp. 23–26 (Burch, 1990); and *The Complete Handbook of Home Brewing*, pp. 43–50 (Miller, 1988).

Consulting Table 2 again, we can look at which specialty malts are used in various styles to get a better idea of the role malt plays in recipe formulation. For instance, we can see that an English bitter has a base of about 92 percent pale ale malt and about 8 percent crystal malt. This style is quite interesting. It has a relatively low gravity (usually between 1.032 and 1.042) and, because not a large amount of malt used, the crystal helps fill the gap by imparting a little bit of caramel sweetness and some extra body, or mouth feel. Together with an aggressive hopping rate, the use of crystal malt in English bitter creates an altogether pleasant blend to imbibe. My prejudice for this style must surely be showing.

In contrast to English bitter, a beer like an imperial stout is quite complex. The range of flavors run from chocolatey to coffeelike to fruity (from the esters present). The crystal gives it some sweetness. The large amount of pale ale malt gives the beer a higher alcohol content, which can be experienced as a slight hot feeling on the tongue. The hop rate is also quite high to help offset the intense malt concentration. Imperial stout is also a quite pleasing beverage, but completely different and very dense in comparison to an English bitter.

Color

We cannot avoid talking about color when we speak of style variation. We touched on the subject earlier when we noted that a pale lager malt gives a lighter straw color while a pale ale malt imparts a more golden hue, but color variations can be made most distinct through the use of specialty malts. I can't think of a better article written on the subject of color in beer than the one by George Fix in the Fall 1988 issue of *zymurgy*. Fix discusses the Lovibond (°L) scale and how it was used as a simple model to match beer or wort samples visually. He says:

> In modern brewing, photometric methods have replaced visual comparison, and the American Society of Brewing Chemists has developed the so-called Standard Reference Method (SRM), which is widely used. Results are expressed as degrees SRM, and for the purposes of this article these units can be regarded as the same as °L (p. 30).

The older Lovibond scale was actually a way of taking existing color samples of beer and comparing them to known color values. For instance, Budweiser has a color value of 2.0°L (SRM) and Michelob Classic Dark has a color value of 17°L. Some comparisons of various malts and their color are given in a table from his article, which is reproduced here as our Table 3. This table shows the range of color from United States 2-row—roughly 1.6°L—to black patent or black barley at a value of roughly 525 °L. We will discuss how to calculate color a little later.

Hops

Just as there are certain areas of the world that are famous for their water, there are also certain hop-growing areas

TABLE 3
Malt Color Chart

Malt Type	Color (°L)
U.S. 2-row	1.4 – 1.8
U.S. 6-row	1.5 – 1.9
Canadian 2-row	1.3 – 1.7
Canadian 6-row	1.4 – 1.9
German pils (2-row)	16
German lager (2-row)	17
Cara-pils	1.3 – 1.8
Wheat malt	1.6 – 1.8
Pale ale	3
Vienna	3 – 5
Light Munich	8 – 11
Dark Munich	18 – 22
Caramel	10 – 120
Chocolate malt	325 – 375
Black	475 – 525
Black barley	500 – 550

which are revered for their contribution to certain styles of beer—from the area of Czechoslovakia where the famous Zatec red or Saaz hops are grown (which contribute a special spicy hoppiness to Pilsner Urquel), to the Yakima Valley in Washington, where many varieties are grown (and some even invented). There are just as many world-famous beers to match. The Hallertauer and Tettnanger areas of Germany are also quite well known as hop-growing regions. I highly recommend the 1990 Special Issue of *zymurgy*, "Hops and Beer," for more information on hops. In this paper, I will focus on hop rates as they pertain to beer styles.

Bittering Properties

Before discussing the relationship of hops to recipe formulation, we should look at the two ways that hops are used
in the brewing process. By boiling the hops for a long period
of time (60 to 90 minutes) you obtain a *bittering* effect from the
hops, and by adding the hops at the very end of a boil (5 to 10
minutes), you get a more *aromatic* element in your beer. You
can also add hops near the end of or after fermentation (known
as "dry hopping") to get a pleasant bouquet.

To match a specific style, you should be aware of the
balance between the bittering and aromatic hops.   Fred
Eckhardt (1989) provides a lot of good information with respect to hop rates, given in International Bittering Units (IBUs).
You can use IBUs to compare your beer with most commercial beers, since information about their hop rates is available
in most cases. Of course, you need to know more than just the
measured amount of hops in beer. You also need to explore
which type of hop attribute is present, bittering or aromatic,
and whether it is appropriate for the style you are brewing.
The AHA provides guidelines for the degree of hoppiness
that should be present for a given style in the "Traditional
Beer Styles" 1991 Special Issue of *zymurgy* and in its annual
National Homebrew Competition guidelines.   Quentin B.
Smith's (1990) article "Matching Hops with Beer Styles" is
also a good reference.

Bitterness is imparted to a beer as a function of how
much alpha acid (and, to a lesser extent, beta acid) is present
in a given hop variety. A hop such as Chinook has a whop-
ping 12 percent alpha acid, while Saaz might be as low as 3.5
to 5 percent alpha acid. We will look at some different hop
varieties now to get a feel for the range available. Table 4 is an
edited version of a table from Bert Grant's article in the 1990
Special Issue of *zymurgy*.

TABLE 4

Hop Varieties

Variety	% Alpha acid	Origin	Comments
Aquila	7.0	U.S.	New, aroma
Banner	10.0	U.S.	New, bitter
Brewers Gold	9.0	U.S./U.K.	Declining use
Bullion	9.0	U.S./U.K.	Declining use
Cascade	5.5	U.S.	Good aroma
Chinook	12.0	U.S.	Recent, bitter
Cluster	7.0	U.S.	Standard
Columbia	10.0	U.S.	Obsolete
Comet	10.0	U.S.	Obsolete
Eroica	10.0	U.S.	Bittering
Fuggles	4.0	U.S./U.K.	Rapidly declining use
Galena	12.0	U.S.	Most popular bittering hop
Goldings	5.0	U.S./Canada	Declining use
Kent Goldings	5.0	U.K.	Declining use
Hallertauer	5.0	U.S./Germany	Declining, premium aroma
Hersbrucker	5.0	U.S./Germany	Aroma
Mt. Hood	5.0	U.S.	Good aroma
Northern Brewer	8.0	U.S./Germany	Bittering
Nugget	12.0	U.S.	Bittering/aroma
Olympic	10.0	U.S.	Obsolete
Perle	8.0	U.S.	Bittering, aroma
Pride of Ringwood	8.0	Australia	Bitter
Saaz	5.0	Czechoslovakia	Premium aroma
Spalt	7.0	Germany	Aroma
Styrian Goldings	6.0	U.S./Yugoslavia	Aroma
Talisman	8.0	U.S.	Declining use
Tettnanger	5.0	U.S./Germany	Aroma
Willamette	5.0	U.S.	Aroma, popularity rapidly increasing
Wye Target	10.0	U.K.	Bitter

We can apply some general rules to selecting hop types when brewing a particular style. If it is a world-recognized beer style, try to use hops that are grown in that area. If they are not available, there might be a U.S. equivalent (assuming the hop isn't from the U.S. in the first place). If none are available, you might try another variety that has similar characteristics to the one you wish to use. Knowing the amount of alpha acid present in your hops and using guidelines found in sources such as Eckhardt (1989) and Jackson (1988), will help to better approximate the style you are trying to brew.

Yeast

On the topic of yeast strains and beer styles, I have found Byron Burch's article in the 1989 Special Issue of *zymurgy* to be the most practical for discussion of yeasts, styles and homebrewing. The merits of dry versus liquid yeast are laid out quickly, with the observation that "It's no accident that most prize-winning beers in major competitions these days use liquid cultures" (p. 55). I wholeheartedly agree—my beers took a giant step forward in quality when I switched from dry packets to liquid strains.* But I think the best part of the article was the strain-by-strain account of the various ale and lager yeasts available. Burch notes the Wyeast and M.eV. Research number equivalent where appropriate. There are great tips on which yeasts work for certain beer styles.

Another resource that is available to homebrewers with respect to yeast types and beer styles is the Winners Circle column in *zymurgy* magazine. I am always curious to see what type of yeast had a hand in producing a beer that was top-rated in competition. Maybe you are too!

---

* Although Whitbread does sell a nice dry ale yeast.

One can make a broad distinction between lager and ale yeasts by observing that typically an ale yeast is a top-fermenting beasty that ferments well between 65 and 75 degrees F (18.5 and 24 degrees C), while a lager yeast is usually bottom fermenting and enjoys the range from 32 to 55 degrees (0 to 13 degrees C). Actually, Gary Bauer (1985) points out a number of traits that differentiate ale yeasts into five different types:

1. Top-fermenting ale yeasts rise to the surface and are removed by skimming.
2. Flocculent ale yeasts, which are in greatest use today, settle to the bottom of the fermenter in a manner similar to lager yeast.
3. Alt bier yeast is a special strain used to produce German-style ales.
4. Weizen bier yeast is a special strain of top-fermenting yeast that produces the characteristic esters found in wheat beer.
5. Strong beer yeast is a top-fermenting yeast similar to wine yeast in its ability to ferment up to an alcohol content of 10 percent by volume (p. 13).

In order to produce beers that are true to their style, at the very least it is worth remembering which type of yeast (ale or lager) should be used. The AHA helps by classifying the 24 style variations into the larger categories of ale or lager in its National Homebrew Competition rules. This listing is worth consulting if you're not sure which yeast should be used for a particular style.

This ends our look at ingredients in beer and the roles they play in recipe formulation. Now we will explore recipe formulation with the aid of a HyperCard stack computer program I created called (surprise) the Recipe Formulator.

THE RECIPE FORMULATOR

When I became interested in more closely targeting specific beer styles, I was amazed at the amount of information available to me (a credit to the hard-working souls whose mission it was to spread the word). There were calculations for water treatment (from Richman, 1989), calculations for extracting the converted sugars from the barley malt (from Burch 1990), calculations for figuring HBU and IBU amounts in hops as a function of hop utilization (from Rager, 1990), and calculations for figuring color in beers (from Fix, 1988). In addition, books that helped define specific beer styles were available from the AHA, and a host of authors have thrown in their two cents as well. I decided to put these calculations together and make a small program that helped me track the various stylistic elements in my brewing. I should stress that these calculations are used for approximations only; there are probably many more factors (how much did I spill?) that contribute to small errors, but I find that the program serves my purposes well.

First, I'll give an overview of what this stack will do. The Recipe Formulator is used by supplying information about your ingredients and conditions via three main cards: Water Treatment, Malt Extraction, and Hop Utilization. The Water Treatment card will (a) display information about famous brewing water; and (b) calculate how much (in grams) of five different ions you need to emulate a specific water style. The Malt Extraction card will (a) calculate gravity yield; (b) give Plato equivalents for specific gravity values (e.g. 1.048 SG = 12 °Plato), and (c) calculate alcohol content by weight and volume. The Hop Utilization card allows you to (a) look at alpha acid values for different hop varieties; and (b) calculate HBU and IBU values. There are two additional cards to help you record notes about the brewing session.

I am going to walk through a recipe that I made recently for one of my favorite beer styles, ordinary bitter. The specific beer I was trying to emulate was one that I enjoyed the last time I found myself in London, Boddington's Bitter. There is a great reference available to help target British bitters and ales called *The Real Ale Drinker's Almanac* (Protz, 1991). It includes information about hop and malt makeup, as well as tasting notes.

Since the water in Portland, Oregon, has the characteristics shown in Table 5 (very soft water), to create a bitter style ale, I needed to do a little work on the water, to help it feel a little more Burtonish. I programmed my stack to accept the ion concentration levels of Portland as a starting point, and then asked it to help me figure out how to better approximate the water in Burton, England (technically I guess it should be Manchester, but what the heck).

TABLE 5
Ion Concentrations (ppm) in Portland, Oregon, Water

Calcium	1.6
Carbonate	2.6
Chloride	2.5
Magnesium	0.57
Potassium	0.25
Sodium	1.5
Sulfate	0.5

Card 1 (p. 92) is a result of my water treatment. I cut and pasted the values for Burton water from Card 2 (p. 93) into the column "What I want it to be" and then asked the stack to calculate the ions and amounts (in grams) I needed to use to treat my water.

Next, I calculated how much grain to add. From *The Real Ale Drinker's Almanac*, I found that Boddington's Bitter is a low-gravity brew (1.035). Its percentages of malt are 95.5

percent pale malt and 1.5 percent patent malt, with 3 percent cane sugar. Having the percentages, I simply plugged in values for what I wanted to brew, mindful of the batch size in gallons, and then fiddled with the amount of grain until I got a close match to my target specific gravity (1.035). Actual gravity yield is calculated according to the following formula:

actual gravity yield = 1 pound of malt x theoretical gravity yield x your efficiency factor

For example, one pound of pale ale malt (which yields a theoretical gravity of 35), multiplied by my efficiency factor (which is 80 percent), gives a gravity yield of 28, so the gravity of my resulting wort would be roughly 1.028. The efficiency factor is found by repeated brewing and observation sessions in which you adjust the theoretical yield toward what you really obtained.

If in the above example my actual gravity ended up being 1.025, I would know that the efficiency factor was not as high as I thought (80 percent), and that it should be adjusted slightly (to 75 percent). The stack uses the information found in Byron Burch's Malt and Sugar Values table (in Burch, 1990) for the theoretical gravity yields, and then calculates the amount of grain needed (in pounds) with the amount of water used (in gallons) to yield your theoretical gravity. On the same card, it calculates the color of the resulting beer in degrees SRM, using the calculation in Fix (1988):

Color (°SRM) = °L x pounds of grain / gallons of water

This calculation gives a good approximation of color, although, as Fix notes, "for darker colored beers this rule can give erratic results" (p. 31). In making this calculation, I assume that nonmalt adjuncts do not play a significant role in coloring a beer. Card 3 (p. 94) helps calculate color and malt extraction. There is also a card called the Grain Warehouse, which is where we can pick and choose from different grain types and adjuncts (Card 4, p. 95).

Similar to the Grain Warehouse, there is a Hop Cold Storage card where we choose which hops will be used (Card 5, p. 96). For the Hop Utilization card (Card 6, p. 97) we supply the amount of hops in ounces and alpha acid content. Hop utilization is determined by a table from "Calculating Hop Bitterness in Beer" (Rager, 1990). An added gravity adjustment (GA) is applied for higher gravity beers (if needed). This is because with high gravity worts (higher than 1.050) there is lower hop utilization. The Recipe Formulator uses the following formula for an IBU (after it converts ounces of hops to grams):

$$IBU = \frac{\text{weight (grams)} \times \% \text{ utilization} \times (\% \text{ alpha acid of hop})}{\text{volume (liters)} \times (1 + GA)}$$

The stack also can store a few pages of notes with the recipe, it includes help on how to use the stack, and it has a Help button for each page. It describes what it expects you to fill in and what it will calculate for you. The stack is dedicated to the authors referenced at the end of this article. Without them, it would not exist. It is available for free.

My desire to brew specific beer styles followed from my appreciation of the various world beer styles, and it is an acknowledgement of the current (and former) master brewers in the world. Their artistry, patience, understanding and ability to manipulate brewing ingredients make beer styles what they are. By trying to emulate the work of masters in the field of brewing, we are keeping the tradition of hand-crafted ales and lagers alive.

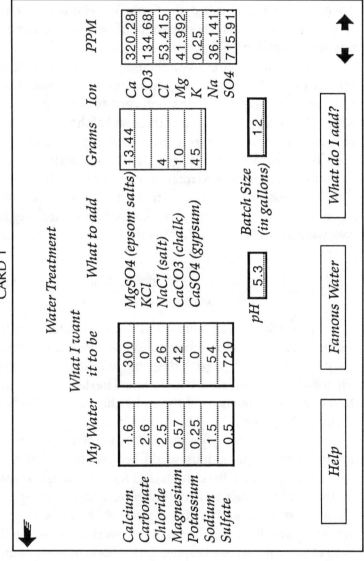

CARD 2

World Brewing Water

	Burton	Dortmund	Dublin	Munich	Pilsen	Vienna
Calcium	300	225	117	75	7	200
Carbonate	0	180	0	150	1.5	120
Chloride	26	60	19	2	5	12
Magnesium	4.2	40	4	18	2	60
Potassium	0	0	0	0	0	0
Sodium	54	60	12	2	2	8
Sulfate	720	120	54	10	5	125

(numbers given are in parts Per Million)

CARD 3

Malt Extraction

Grist List	# lbs.	°L	Extract Potential	Color Result	Target Garvity	Extract Efficiency
Pale Malt	15	1.6	3.5	2	4.5	0.75
Crystal Malt	.25	4.0	2.0	0.833333	0.75	
Demerara Sugar	.5	1	4.5	0.041667	1.5	
				2.875	47.25	

Gravity Yield

1.04725
x 0.75
- - - - - -
1.035438

British Gravity		Plato	Date Recorded
OSG	1035	8.75	4-2-92
RSG	1012	3	4-14-92
TSG	1006	1.5	4-18-92

Alcohol Percentage by

weight	*volume*
3.021075	3.79447

Help	Gravity	Alcohol

CARD 4

Grain Warehouse

Name	°L	extract potential
Pale Malt	1.6	3.5
Lager Malt	1.6	3.5
Munich Malt	.7	2.5
Mild Ale Malt	2.0	3.0
Crystal Malt	2.0	2.0
Crystal Malt	4.0	2.0
Crystal Malt	8.0	2.0
Wheat Malt	4	3.0
Dextrine Malt	3.2	2.8
Others...		
Malt Extract		3.6
Dry Malt		4.5
Corn Sugar		3.6
Cane Sugar		4.5
Brown Sugar		4.5
Rice Syrup		3.6
Dextrine Powder		4.5

Our Brew Needs...

Name	lbs	°L	extract potential
Pale Malt	1.5	1.6	3.5
Crystal Malt	2.5	4.0	2.0
Demerara Sugar	.5	1	4.5

CARD 5

Hop Cold Storage

Hop Type	Alpha	Beta
Brewers Gold	9.0	9.3
Bullion	9.0	9.2
Cascade	5.5	5.9
Chinook	12.0	13.2
Cluster	7.0	7.4
Eroica	10.0	10.5
Fuggles	4.0	4.2
Galena	12.0	12.5
Goldings	5.0	5.2
Kent Goldings	5.0	5.2
Hallertauer	5.0	5.3
Hersbrucker	5.0	5.2
Mt. Hood	5.0	5.3
Northern Brewer	8.0	8.8
Nugget	12.0	13.0
Perle	8.0	8.2
Saaz	5.0	5.2
Spalt	7.0	7.4
Tettnanger	5.0	5.2
Willamette	5.0	5.4

Our Brew Needs...

Hop Type	oz.	Alpha	Beta
Fuggles	1	4.0	4.2
Goldings	1	5.0	5.2
Northern Brewer	1	8.0	8.8
Kent Goldings	1	5.0	5.2

CARD 6

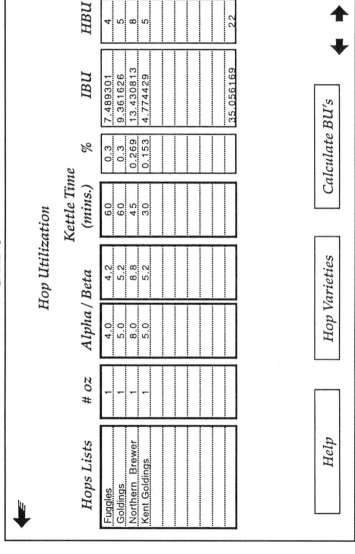

Hop Utilization

Hops Lists	# oz	Alpha / Beta		Kettle Time (mins.)	%	IBU	HBU
Fuggles	1	4.0	4.2	6.0	0.3	7.489301	4
Goldings	1	5.0	5.2	6.0	0.3	9.361626	5
Northern Brewer	1	8.0	8.8	4.5	0.269	13.430813	8
Kent Goldings	1	5.0	5.2	3.0	0.153	4.774429	5
						35.056169	22

Help   Hop Varieties   Calculate BU's

Doug Henderson has been involved with computers and type-setting for the last 10 years. This passion has translated to home-brewing, and he has been actively pursuing the mythical perfect Pilsener and pale ale for the past six years. In addition to playing with style variations in brewing, he has been a member of the Oregon Brew Crew for the past three years. He is currently serving as newsletter editor for the Crew and is an active certified beer judge.

REFERENCES

Bauer, G. (1985). The influences of raw materials on the production of all-grain beers. *zymurgy,* 8:4, 9-13.

Briggs, D. E., Hough, J. S., Stevens, R., and Young, T. W. (1981). *Malting and Brewing Science, Vols. I and II.* New York, N.Y.: Chapman and Hall.

Burch, B. (1989). Of yeasts and beer styles. *zymurgy,* 12:4, 55-57, 63.

Burch, B. (1990). *Brewing Quality Beers.* Fulton, Calif.: Joby Books.

Eckhardt, F. (1989). *The Essentials of Beer Style.* Portland, Ore.: Fred Eckhardt Associates.

Fix, G. (1988). Beer color evaluation. *zymurgy,* 11:3, 30–33.

Fix, G. (1989). *Principles of Brewing Science.* Boulder, Colo.: Brewers Publications.

Foster, T. (1990). *Pale Ale.* Boulder, Colo.: Brewers Publications.

Hops and Beer (1990). [Special Issue]. *zymurgy,* 13:4.

Grant, B. (1990). Hop varieties and qualities. *zymurgy,* 13:4, 24–26.

Jackson, M. (1988). *The New World Guide to Beer.* Philadelphia: Running Press.

Line, D. (1985). *Big Book of Brewing.* Herts, England: Argus Books Ltd.

Miller, D. (1988). *The Complete Handbook of Home Brewing.* Pownal, Vt.: Storey Communications, Inc.

Miller, D. (1990). *Continental Pilsener.* Boulder, Colo.: Brewers Publications.

Noonan, G. J. (1986). *Brewing Lager Beer.* Boulder, Colo.: Brewers Publications.

Papazian, C. (1991). *The New Complete Joy of Home Brewing.* New York: Avon Books.

Protz, R. (1991). *The Real Ale Drinker's Almanac.* Moffat, Scotland: Lochar Publishing.

Richman, D. (1989). Water treatment: how to calculate salt adjustment. *zymurgy,* 12:5, 29–32.
Rager, J. (1990). Calculating hop bitterness in beer. *zymurgy,* 13:4, 53–54.
Smith, Q. B. (1990). Matching hops with beer styles. *zymurgy,* 13:4, 55–60.
Traditional Beer Styles (1991). [Special Issue]. *zymurgy,* 14:4.

7. Breaking Out of Beginning Brewing

Don Hoag and John Judd
Brewmasters, Northern Ale Stars Homebrewers Guild

Just what is a "beginner"? After consulting with the AHA staff, we concluded that the typical novice brewer attending the AHA National Homebrew Conference is probably pretty serious about brewing, has brewed several times already, and knows enough to ignore extract label instructions to add sugar and not boil the wort. We figure this person has the basic process down for extract brewing and is aware of the importance of sanitation and how to achieve it.

So where do we start? There is no single thing that the novice can or should do to move into more advanced brewing. We do not intend to cover such topics as yeast culturing and management, or mashing from grain, at length. Plenty of information and instructions on these and other such topics are already available. We will instead offer advice, tips, and descriptions of some procedures we use that can enhance the

John Judd (left) and Don Hoag (right)

quality of your beer and, in some cases, make the brewing process a little easier. This information will also give you more control over the resulting beer, which is what breaking out of beginning is all about. We will discuss some topics related to ingredients first, and then move on to the areas of techniques and equipment.

INGREDIENTS

Chapter 5 in this book is dedicated entirely to the topic of improving extract beers, so we will not discuss extracts. We would like, however, to offer one tip related to malt. Even if they haven't tried it, most novice brewers are probably aware that they can use relatively small amounts of specialty malts with their extracts to impart color and flavor to their beer. We have found that you get more out of such malts if they are crushed before they are added to the water. Because the amounts are small, crushing does not need to be a big job requiring a grain mill. A rolling pin will work, although it can be messy. A quick grind using an electric coffee grinder will give you pretty good results, although you should be careful not to overgrind and produce flour. Once the grain is ground, we usually sift it to get rid of the fine flour and dust. Just bounce it up and down in a stainless-steel strainer a few times. After sifting, we put the crushed malt in a hop bag or cheese-cloth bag. It is then very easy to remove the grain at the desired time—just scoop out the bag with a spoon.

When hopping the wort, you have the choice of several forms of hops. Pellet hops are great for convenience and they tend to keep longer, as there is less surface area exposed to air. It is a little difficult, however, to remove the hops from the wort prior to fermentation. We have found that a plastic funnel with a screen, available from many homebrew suppliers, works well to strain out the "sludge" from pellets. A strong rationale for straining out this sludge was mentioned by George Fix at the conference in Milwaukee. He indicated that if you are reusing yeast from batch to batch, it is particularly important to remove the vegetable matter from the wort. The only problem with the straining system we use is that the screens are almost too fine, so it is handy to have a helper when you are pouring. The helper can continuously scrape a metal spoon across the screen, allowing the liquid to pass. It probably will be necessary at times to stop pouring, and scrape away and dispose of the sludge buildup. One alternative is to force-cool the wort to achieve a good cold break, and siphon it out of the kettle. We will discuss this process at greater length when discussing cooling the wort.

Dry hopping is another area of concern to some brewers,

who worry about the potential for contamination from hops, clogging blow-off tubes, and other problems. We have avoided these problems by using a kind of "hop back" approach. When pouring the hot wort into the fermenter, we place a quantity of fresh leaf hops into a colander and pour the wort through that. If you have a colander with fine holes that cause the beer to flow fairly slowly, and are using a good quality aroma hop, this is a simple way to pick up some nice aromatic qualities from the hops without going to the trouble of dry hopping.

As a final note, we'd like to pass on a recommendation from a friend of ours in Chicago who says that he takes a little plastic bottle of hop oil to ball games. A couple of drops in his cup makes the mass-produced beer available at the stadium much more enjoyable!

Yeast is another critical ingredient for the novice brewer to increase his or her knowledge of and sophistication about. Again, there is an entire chapter in this volume (Chapter 15) devoted to this topic so we won't provide a great amount of detail on it here. We have been using liquid cultures for several years, but for most of the past eight years that we have taught a formal homebrew course we used what was usually a dependable dried yeast for the introductory brewing demonstration. Then, after the dried yeast let us down in our class last year, we decided to teach our students to use the liquid cultures right away. Relatively simple techniques can be followed with great success. We recommend using a starter culture to build up the amount of viable yeast. First, follow the instructions on the foil packet to start the culture. Prepare a starter by boiling 2 to 3 tablespoons of dry malt extract and a couple of hop pellets together for 20 minutes, then force-cool this small amount of wort in a cold water bath. When cooled, pour it into a sanitized container (we have a laboratory flask, but bottles or small jars work equally well). After the foil yeast packet has become swollen, tear it open and pour its contents into the wort. Affix a cap, shake vigorously to aerate it, then replace the cap with an airlock after shaking. In two to three days, the yeast will have worked on the fresh malt. Once the vigorous fermentation subsides, it is ready for pitching. By building up the volume of yeast you are pitching, your homebrews will begin to ferment much more quickly. This decreases the risk of contamination considerably.

Other than inconvenience, the biggest drawback to using liquid cultures is cost. We follow fairly simple techniques to harvest yeast for reuse. After primary fermentation has been completed, we pour some of the yeast sediment from the bottom of the fermenter into a few small, sanitized glass jars and cap immediately. These can be stored in the refrigerator and reused (the length of time they can be stored varies with the yeast strain, but a couple of weeks to a month is not uncommon for us). We have had no problems with contamination using these methods, even though they are not very sophisticated. If you are concerned, you can increase your own sophistication in yeast culturing and management. Or, you can use starter cultures for the second and subsequent generations of yeast. This gives you a chance to inspect the yeast's action before pitching. If it appears to be fermenting well and smells clean and beery, you don't have much to worry about. By following good sanitation procedures, you can easily ferment enough batches from a single liquid yeast packet to reduce the cost to the that of dried yeasts (or less).

The final ingredient we will discuss is water, which makes up by far the largest percentage of the final product. We are not scientists and have no desire to be, so we follow a simple rule: if the water tastes good, it will probably make good beer. However, this is another area in which the novice homebrewer, through increased knowledge, can exert more control over the brewing process. At a minimum, we recommend that you obtain an analysis of your water for hardness, pH, mineral content and the like. You can then consult the number of sources available that discuss the appropriate water profile for particular beer styles, and follow their recommendations for adjusting the water to move toward the desired profile. We obtained an analysis from our municipal water department, whose chemist was happy to help us interpret it.

EQUIPMENT AND TECHNIQUES

If you continue brewing, it is likely that someday you will want to try mashing. When you do, keep in mind that there are several options available. We have used an English Bru-Heat for the past seven years. This unit consists of a 7-gallon (U.S.) plastic pail with spigot, an electric thermostatically controlled heating element, and a grain bag that fits inside the pail. Water is heated inside the unit and the ground grain is stirred into the water to form the mash. The unit was designed to mash with the grain bag inside the pail, but we soon discovered this leads to poor temperature control, and now do not use the grain bag while mashing. If you try the Bru-Heat method, remember that it is possible to burn the grain on the heating element. When you turn up the thermostat to boost the heat, you should stir the mash regularly to prevent burning.

The Bru-Heat may be used to do single-temperature or upward step mashes. At the end of the mash, it can be used to slowly boost the temperature to 170 degrees F (76.5 degrees C) for mashing off (again, be careful to stir). Because we do not use the grain bag inside the Bru-Heat, we must then transfer the mash to a separate lauter-tun. The Bru-Heat is convenient,

Homebrewers found new and interesting ways to imbibe their favorite beverage at one of the hospitality suites.

but it is not cheap. You might consider splitting the cost with another brewer, and sharing the unit.

It is possible to mash in a large pot on the stove top, but we don't recommend this method because temperature control is a problem. Stove burners do not maintain a particular temperature well and therefore require almost constant monitoring and adjusting.

Probably the easiest and least expensive alternative to the Bru-Heat is a picnic cooler. We have experimented with several types and shapes. The cylindrical beverage cooler is the best, because you are assured that it has a food-grade plastic interior. To mash in a cooler, heat the water on the stove to strike temperature (about 15 to 20 degrees above the desired mash temperature). After pouring the water into the cooler and adding the grain, you will be close to your target. Small quantities of cold water may be added if the resulting temperature is too high. If it is too low, you can remove some of the liquid from the cooler, boil it, and return it to the cooler. This same "decoction" method can be used for upward step mashes in the cooler.

Sparging the sweet wort from the mash requires some simple but specialized equipment. We use the nested bucket method described in *The New Complete Joy of Home Brewing* (Papazian, 1991). A pair of 5-gallon food-grade pails and a plastic spigot are all you need. Try to find buckets that previously contained mild or inert products such as frosting or malt syrup from a bakery. You will never get the pickle smell out of a pickle pail! About 1 1/2 to 2 inches above the bottom of the outside bucket, drill a 3/4-inch hole and install a plastic spigot and o-rings, available in any hardware store. In the bottom of the inner bucket, drill numerous small holes to form a mesh through which the wort may be drained. After the buckets are nested, we place the grain bag inside to aid in the filtration process. This helps us avoid problems with stuck sparges or grain particles clogging the holes. Grain bags may be purchased from suppliers independent of the Bru-Heat. We use bungee cords to secure the grain bag to the bucket.

In order to speed up the sparging process, we heat the sparge water to 170 degrees F (76.5 degrees C) in our brew kettle while we are mashing in the Bru-Heat. When the mash is transferred to the lauter-tun, we rinse out the Bru-Heat and transfer the hot water into it. We are then ready to begin sparging immediately. To transfer hot liquid safely, we use a saucepan to bail the liquid.

For boiling, the obvious choice is to use kitchen equipment you already possess. We began our brewing with a

Revere Ware stainless-steel pot, and then bought enamelled canning pots. However, in order to mash, or to do a full wort boil with an extract beer, you will need a boiling kettle large enough to hold at least 7 gallons. You start by boiling 5 1/2 to 6 gallons of wort (which reduces to 5 gallons during the boil through evaporation), and you need some head space in the kettle. We use a converted stainless-steel Sankey-style beer keg. Although commercial brewers and beer distributors may hate us, this is an excellent kettle. However, *you must observe safety precautions when adapting kegs for your use.* The empty keg is actually filled with carbon dioxide or air that has displaced the beer. You must relieve the pressure carefully before dismantling the valve assembly. This is most easily done by tapping the keg (making sure any source of gas is turned off) and opening the spigot to vent the gas or air. Only when the keg is truly empty should you think about trying to take it apart. After the keg is safely taken apart, the top must be cut off. You probably will want to leave one of the handles on it. If you are not mechanically inclined and do not want to tackle this project, you can find 8-gallon enamelled pots that do quite well as kettles.

Whether or not you are mashing, doing a full wort boil means you will have to force-cool the wort somehow. The faster you bring the wort to the pitching temperature, the less risk there is for contamination. You will also benefit from having a good cold break, which means less trub and potential off-flavors in your beer. There are two broad classes of wort chillers available to homebrewers. These were profiled in *zymurgy* Vol. 15, No. 1 (Goeres & Goeres, 1992), and are discussed in Chapter 9 of this book. One type is the counterflow chiller, in which hot wort flows through a tube surrounded by cold water flowing in the opposite direction in a larger tube. The other type is the immersion chiller, in which a copper coil is immersed in the hot wort and cold water is run through the coil. In our experience, you get the most rapid cooling when the coil is agitated in the hot wort, which also helps aerate it.

We don't use either type; instead, we use the Lake Superior wort chiller. Living in Duluth, Minnesota, on the shore of this great lake provides us with a year-round source of *cold* tap water. We merely set our brew kettle in a cold bath of water, and change the water after about 15 minutes. After a total immersion time of 30 to 45 minutes, the wort is at a suitable temperature for pitching. There are two major advantages to this approach. First, we do not have to transfer the wort through a chiller which must be sanitized. Second, the wort is not agitated during cooling. This means that the trub which has coagulated drops to the bottom. We merely siphon the clearer wort off this sediment into our fermenter.

Once the wort is in the fermenter, it must be agitated. This aerates it, which is advantageous for quick yeast action. It also mixes it fully, so that the hydrometer reading is accurate. In our early years of extract brewing, we did not completely mix the wort with cold water, and false readings resulted.

Beginning brewers may start out with a kit that includes a 7-gallon food-grade plastic fermenter. The trouble with these is that we've always suspected plastic of being permeable to air. Secondly, vigorous cleaning can result in scratches on the inside surface, which may harbor bacteria or other contaminants. What you want in a fermenter is something that will hold the entire amount of wort, is as airtight as possible, and can be easily cleaned and sanitized. Glass carboys are probably the most common fermenter, and meet most of our criteria. The problem, of course, is that glass is easily broken by impact or through sudden temperature changes (don't pour your boiling hot wort into a cold carboy!).

If we had written this article three years ago, we would have been able to brag that we had never broken a carboy. No longer.... But we do still use them. Use care in cleaning and rinsing, soaking when possible to avoid overhandling. And invest in a carboy handle—you won't be sorry.

The other fermenting vessel that meets all of our criteria is constructed of stainless steel. Two of the most easily accessible are Sankey beer kegs and 5-gallon soda kegs. We use Sankey quarter barrels to ferment 5-gallon batches. *NOTE: the previous warning about kegs under pressure applies here as well!* Do not dismantle any keg without first venting it. Once it is safe to take apart, you can remove the valve assembly and use a No. 11 rubber cork (drilled) with an airlock to adapt it for use as a fermenter. This is a great fermenter—you can soak it clean, it won't break, and you don't have to worry about a blow-off tube because the keg is large enough to hold the head during primary fermentation. Soda kegs are frequently used for dispensing by homebrewers, but may also be used as fermenters. We tend to use them as secondary fermenters, transferring beers from carboys to these to condition. We remove the center of the gas inlet valve and affix a length of plastic tubing with the other end in a bucket of water to act as an airlock.

One further consideration related to fermenters is maintaining a cool temperature during the primary fermentation of lagers. Homebrewers frequently forget that among the byproducts of fermentation (in addition to alcohol and carbon dioxide) is heat. To dissipate this heat, we place the fermentation vessel in a cold water bath during its primary fermentation phase. This prevents the temperature from rising too high and causing undesirable esters in lagers.

And finally, here are some miscellaneous tips. First, if you are doing a full wort boil in a modified keg/kettle, you will eventually have to pick it up and pour the hot wort, even if you bail most of it. We have found that using a small C-clamp as a hook to hold and tilt the hot bottom of the keg works well and prevents burns. Second, we exclusively use wooden paddles to stir the mash and wort. These have long enough handles to minimize the risk of burns. Usually you can obtain them for a very reasonable price from a restaurant supply house. Finally, we advise a couple of techniques for bottling. Our standard bench capper has been fitted with a rubber cushion on the top surface of the base. This serves to absorb excess pressure when the caps are crimped on the bottle, reducing the possibility of breakage. We also recommend wearing a leather glove on the hand that holds the bottle during the capping action. It will help prevent cuts should the bottle break.

Some of you may have observed that our brewing technique involves frequent transfer of the wort or beer via siphoning. We do not use the water-filled hose or any other artificial technique to start the siphon. Instead, we rely on our mouths. Of course, you are aware of the fact that the human mouth is full of bacteria. To reduce the risk of contamination, we employ a dose of distilled spirits vigorously forced about the mouth and lips to sanitize the siphon priming mechanism. Our personal favorites are citrus- or pepper-flavored vodka, or dill-flavored Akvavit from Denmark.

Don Hoag and John Judd have been homebrewing together for more than 10 years. They are founding members and past presidents of the Northern Ale Stars Homebrewers Guild, Minnesota's oldest homebrew club. They have won ribbons in several national and regional competitions, including blue ribbons awarded by the AHA and HWBTA. They have contributed articles to zymurgy, and, through their local community education program, they have taught more than 100 students to homebrew over the past eight years. Hoag and Judd share a lifetime membership to the AHA. Both are members of Britain's Campaign for Real Ale (Judd is a lifetime member), and Hoag has served on the AHA Board of Advisors since its inception. In their other lives, Judd works as a senior economic development planner for a regional development commission, while Hoag is a human resources advisor for an international crude-oil pipeline company.

REFERENCES

Goeres, R., and Goeres, M. (1992). Wort chillers: Three styles to improve your brew. *zymurgy*, 15:1, 38-39.

Papazian, C. (1991). *The New Complete Joy of Home Brewing*. New York: Avon Books.

8. Breathing New Life into Your Homebrew Club

*

Thom Tomlinson
President, Hop, Barley & the Ale'rs

If you and your friends already brew together, why start a homebrew club? If you already participate in a homebrew club, why do you feel concerned when your club grows a little sluggish? For that matter, why do your active members continue to participate? If your club desires new blood, have you thought about why those who are reticent about joining should find the time and the dues money to do so? Careful consideration of these questions reveals many benefits of starting, participating in or rejuvenating a homebrew club.

Most homebrewers know that sharing their creations with friends who have brewed their own enhances the enjoyment of homebrewing. The friendships that develop out of such gatherings are themselves enough of a reason to join a

115

Thom Tomlinson

club. What can a club offer in addition to the incentive of friendly gatherings and shared homebrew? Imagine for a moment the number of different beers that two brewing friends can produce in a year. Now think about the variety of flavors that those two friends can experience in a year. The more flavors they experience, the more they improve the sensory capabilities of their palates and noses. Improved sensory skills will enhance their enjoyment of beer. Certainly a person will taste more different beers, and thus flavors, in a club than in a small circle of brewers.

In addition, homebrew clubs offer the opportunity to learn about the many different styles of beer. Left to their own devices, homebrewers would probably learn as much as possible about their favorite style of beer. When you participate in a club you are exposed to all the other brewers' knowledge of their favorite styles, which increases your knowledge of styles in general.

There are many reasons to join a homebrew club or to get one started in your area. This paper focuses on five important processes for starting or rejuvenating a homebrew club: (1) organizing a club, (2) getting members and keeping them involved, (3) financing a new club or raising money for an existing one, (4) types of meetings and meeting formats and (5) suggestions for special events. Most of the ideas presented here arose from conversations with members of homebrew clubs around the United States and from my experience as president of Hop, Barley & the Ale'rs.

ORGANIZING A HOMEBREW CLUB

Goals

Anyone who has ever worked with a group of people knows that it is a rare event when everyone is in agreement. Even if everyone can agree on a goal, each individual might see a different way to reach it. For this reason it is extremely important for your group to establish a club purpose. You might choose to do this by verbal agreement. For example, at your organizational meeting those in attendance may decide that the club will provide an opportunity to taste each other's beer. That in and of itself can be a club's purpose and its goal. You may decide to learn more about beer by evaluating each other's beers. In that case you have identified an educational component of your club's purpose. Such informal goals will help the club members know what to expect from the club.

Your club may decide to establish a more formal set of goals in the form of club bylaws. Bylaws specifically state the purpose of the club and provide some guidelines on how to accomplish its goals. Remember, when deciding on the club's purpose select those aspects that everyone agrees upon. The bylaws of Hop, Barley & The Ale'rs contain four simple purposes:

1. To engage in enjoyable social activities focused on homebrewing as a common foundation.

2. To learn more about beer, beer tasting, beer judging and brewing techniques, based on sharing knowledge and experience.

3. To promote the hobby and enjoyment of homebrewing.

4. To promote the responsible use and enjoyment of alcoholic beverages.

Bylaws also provide a framework for establishing membership, voting rights, responsibilities of officers, procedures for deciding on the amount of dues and how to collect them, and a procedure for making changes in the bylaws. Furthermore, a written framework has the advantage of remaining clear and constant across time. Your club may not want to write a set of bylaws; however, if you choose to, an example appears in the Appendix.

Meeting Location

After you have established your operating procedures you will need to decide on a meeting location. If space permits, you can hold meetings at the homes of your members. This works for the Sonoma Beerocrats of Santa Rosa, California. Every other month they have between 50 and 60 members attend a social meeting at the home of a member. On the other months they meet at a home of a member or at Great Fermentations, the local homebrew supply store. The Birmingham Brewmasters of Alabama also hold their meetings at the local homebrew supply shop. Other clubs have the good fortune of being able to meet in a brewpub, a microbrewery or a local bar. Hop, Barley & the Ale'rs presently meets in the conference room of a local inn; however, they have held meetings in a brewery, in a Jaycee hall, at an Elk's lodge, at a member's house, and in a stand of trees in the Rocky Mountains.

You may encounter some difficulty in finding a suitable location, but persist in your search. In the case of Hop, Barley & the Ale'rs it took a year of moving around, constantly calling local businesses, and the help of a friendly local business person to find a regular meeting place. Having a regular meeting location helps bring in new members and will assist your advertising efforts.

MEMBERS

Recruiting New Members

Why should a club want to bring in new members? First of all, a club, like any other group of people, is dynamic. That means that the club consists of individuals in interpersonal relationships and that it exists in a constant state of flux. Members may leave the club for one reason or another and relationships within the club will grow and change. When you bring in new members you help maintain the dynamic nature of the group by replacing lost members and by adding another human variable to the existing relationships.

A second, excellent reason to bring in new members is to increase the number of people interested in homebrewing. More homebrewers means a need for more supply shops, which can lead to a competitive marketplace with lower prices. Furthermore, with more people brewing their own beer and developing an appreciation for the many faces of beer, local microbreweries and brewpubs will stand a better chance of succeeding and continuing to provide us all with an option to generic, commercial beer.

Clubs use many different strategies to bring in new members. One popular way to introduce people to homebrewing, and to bring in new club members, is to have a brewing demonstration. Hop, Barley & the Ale'rs holds a regular homebrewing demonstration at a local eatery. About 50 people attend each of these demonstrations, and the club picks up new members each time. You might try holding a brewing demonstration at a local bar, restaurant, county fair or at an advertised meeting of the club.

Some clubs bring in new faces by advertising their meetings in local brewing newspapers. For example, Brewers United 4 Real Potables (BURP) advertises in *The Barley Corn,* a newspaper devoted to brewing news. A less expensive, but definitely effective, option is to post signs in local brew shops. This type of advertising reaches a specific group who will most likely have an interest in your club, though it does not reach the person who has never brewed a batch of beer. Advertising in pubs and microbreweries will reach people with an interest in good beer and people who have never brewed. Of course, the age-old saying is true—word of mouth is the best advertisement. If your members are happy they will tell their friends, who will then visit a meeting, and before you know it you will have new members.

A radio show about homebrewing provides a unique way to spread the homebrew bug. Jerry Bourbonnais of the Boreal Bottlers in Bemidji, Minnesota, hosts a monthly show devoted to homebrew. You may not be able to get your own radio show, but look into the possibility of speaking on a local talk show or public interest station.

Hop, Barley & the Ale'rs takes advantage of local special events (e.g., street festivals, beer festivals) to advertise the club in a very effective way. Since the club meets at a regular site and on the same night in each month (fourth Tuesday) the members can make up batches of cards advertising the location and night of their meetings. A group of members then attends the event and talks to people about homebrewing, making sure to leave each contact with a card. At the 1991 Great American Beer Festival the members wore brightly colored buttons reading "Ask Me About Homebrew." You might be surprised at how many people will stop you to ask about homebrew! The combination of buttons and cards is an extremely inexpensive and effective way to advertise your club.

Keeping Members Involved

Once you have a club how can you keep the members involved? How do you spread the responsibility of maintaining the membership so that one or two people do not grow tired of handling the operations? Keeping a club running may require very little effort or a great effort; it depends upon the goals of the club and the number of members. Responsibilities such as mailing announcements or a newsletter, buying T-shirts and finding a meeting location, in addition to handling operations, can become overwhelming if continuously left to one person. Spreading these responsibilities around may be the most difficult task in the life of a homebrew club.

In order to keep members actively involved it is important to establish a sense of club pride. The sense of unity and professionalism that can develop in a club promotes a real desire to participate. You can establish club pride in several ways: by appealing to a sense of community spirit, by sharing high-quality homebrew or by doing well—individually or as a club—in homebrew competitions. You have to tailor the process of building pride to the needs of your club, but the importance of maintaining strong ties to the community cannot be overstated. A club that interacts with the community, providing services or information, will survive and thrive. The club will receive positive feedback from the community, adding to the pride and enthusiasm of its members. When members are proud of their club they will remain active and even help assume some of the responsibilities of operation.

Another way to keep members active and help spread

The Abnormal Brewers of Normal, Illinois, were one of many homebrew clubs that made their presence known at this year's conference.

around the responsibility is to establish manager positions. You might appoint a member with a flair for graphics or sales to the position of Advertising Manager. You might ask the member with the most yeast culturing experience to manage the club's yeast bank. Many clubs have Merchandise Managers whose primary responsibility is to purchase and sell club merchandise. Once your club is established you may want to purchase kegs or other brewing equipment and elect a Technical Manager to assume responsibility for its care and maintenance. Another frequently created position is that of Food Manager or Burgermeister, who is responsible for coordinating the food served at meetings. Remember to recognize all your managers in your newsletter.

Creating committees provides another avenue for getting members involved. When planning special events ask members who are not officers to be on the committee. Sometimes you may need to gently encourage members to head special event committees; however, members almost always get enthusiastic when organizing a club function.

Finally, if you really want to keep your members interested, make sure that the club continues to do what the members want. Do not let your officers distance themselves from the membership. This may not be a problem for small clubs, but as your club grows in size it might become more difficult. It frequently happens that a small group of brewers starts a club, assumes operating responsibilities or officer positions and in general runs the club. That is fine in the beginning, but as the club grows, so should the number of people who are integrated into its operation.

The officers and club managers can keep members involved by discussing club business with them. Talk with new members, old members, or members who have not attended with regularity, and ask them what they want from the club.

Issue a standing invitation for members to attend officer meetings and make sure your newsletter contains all decisions made by the officers. Keeping your members informed and listening to their ideas will make everyone a happy camper.

MONEY

Financing The Club

Money makes the world go 'round. Well, maybe not, but it sure makes life a little easier, especially for a homebrew club. You will need money to print and mail a newsletter, to provide essentials for club gatherings, and maybe even to pay for a monthly meeting location. The amount of money that you need for a year depends on the goals and interests of your club. Likewise, how you raise the necessary funds will depend on your club.

Most clubs charge members yearly dues ranging from $5 to $30. If your operating budget is small, you may not need any additional funding, but most clubs do engage in other activities designed to generate revenue. A popular idea is to sell merchandise bearing the club's logo, such as T-shirts, mugs, bar towels and brewing aprons. Clubs with newsletters have the option of selling advertising. Hop, Barley & the Ale'rs raised about $350 in advertising sales over the last year. Breweries, pubs, restaurants, importers and homebrew shops are all candidates for advertising.

Corporate sponsorship also provides an avenue of support for clubs. Many clubs have sponsors who provide a meeting place, and some clubs have restaurant sponsors who offer a location for special events such as a chili cook-off or beer tasting. Some clubs arrange for donations of beer for commercial tastings or food for special events. Hop, Barley &

the Ale'rs recently received sponsorship money from a local restaurant in exchange for providing a brewing demonstration every other month. The club benefits by getting the money and new members, and the restaurant benefits by increasing its bar business and strengthening its image as an establishment interested in promoting good beer. Check the businesses in your area and look for a win-win situation.

A more direct method of raising money is a fundraiser or raffle. Hop, Barley & the Ale'rs raised over $800 auctioning used brewing equipment, brewery T-shirts and caps, beer tastings, dental check-ups and brewing consultations. Members and local businesses donated all the merchandise and services. The brewing consultations were particularly fun— the members bid for the right to brew and split an all-grain batch with one of the club's more experienced brewers. The brewers in BURP hold a monthly raffle of items donated by breweries, distributors and importers. They have successfully amassed quite a treasury using this method. When you plan a fundraising event, check your local laws; in some places raffles or auctions require a special permit or license.

Managing The Club's Finances

Once you decide how much money you need, how do you go about managing the money in the treasury? The treasury provides two functions for a homebrew club: (1) it accounts for the inflow and outflow of money, and (2) it provides financial information for making club decisions. A simple and direct method of organizing your treasury is to record all monetary transactions in one of two ledgers. This is really like keeping two checkbooks. One is used to record all cash (currency) transactions, and is supported by a cash receipts book. The other ledger lists all the checks written on behalf of the club, which are handled through the club's checking account. This account will also include records of deposits and checks written to cover club expenses.

Activity from each of the two ledgers is summarized on an income statement, which reflects the inflow of cash (revenues from dues, merchandise sales, advertising sales, etc.) and the outflow of cash (expenses such as newsletter mailing costs and merchandise purchases). By subtracting the total expenses from the total revenues you can determine the club's operating income (if the difference is positive) or operating loss (if the difference is negative).

Clubs usually like to project a fiscal year's (January to December for Hop Barley & the Ale'rs) operating expenses each December. They project costs for the meeting room, monthly newsletter and special events, and any other expense that occurs on an annual basis. After estimating the year's operating costs the club can get to the task of raising the needed funds. Before engaging in new enterprises or buying equipment for the club, Hop Barley & the Ale'rs makes sure that the operating expenses have been met. By following the simple strategy of determining your needs for a year, projecting expenses for attaining those needs, and not spending money on other items or events until the operating budget is met, your club will never end a year with an operating loss.

MEETING FORMATS AND ACTIVITIES

What do you do at your meetings? If your club has been around a while, how do you jazz up those predictable meetings? An array of activities, many of which cost only small sums of money, are at the disposal of most clubs. Before reviewing suggestions for club activities, consider the type of meeting that you would like to attend.

Which works best, meetings with a regular format or meetings without a defined organization? Again, it depends on your club. Some clubs gather for a social meeting and do not have an agenda. Other clubs gather with specific events in mind; for example, the Birmingham Brewmasters got together and watched the Beerhunter series by Michael Jackson. Most clubs, whether or not their meetings are structured, have some expectations about what will happen at the meeting.

Hop, Barley & the Ale'rs provides an example of a club with a regular meeting format. Meetings take place at the same location on the fourth Tuesday of every month. Meetings begin at 7 p.m. with members gathering to eat and socialize. At about 7:20 they discuss club business; this consists of bringing the members up to date on decisions made at the officers' meeting. Trying to make decisions at meetings with 60 to 80 people can be quite difficult, so try to hold officers' meetings on a different night. After discussing business and bringing everyone up to date on current brewing events, the members continue to socialize and eat. By 8 p.m. everyone grabs a seat and prepares for a guest speaker. The list of candidates for speaking at a homebrew club is virtually endless. You might bring in professional brewers, experts with some procedure or technical equipment, businesses involved in the brewing industry, travel agents or touring companies willing to present a slide show on tours of England or Germany. The speaker section of the agenda can even include a presentation of homebrewing gadgets designed by members.

During the last hour of their meetings Hop Barley & the Ale'rs does what every other club in the world does—taste each other's beer! Each month highlights a different style, thus exposing the members to a wide range of beer styles. A member of the club brews a keg of beer in the style of the month and members bring their own efforts at that or any other style. Every other month the style is in conjunction with AHA Club Only Competition. Every month the members vote on the best representative of that month's style with the winning recipe appearing in the monthly newsletter.

Other clubs have different activities and schedules. The Sonoma Beerocrats hold a social meeting one month and a technical or how-to meeting the next. BURP practices judging its style of the month, giving members an opportunity to learn about the characteristics of each style. The Carolina Brewmasters meet on Saturdays and brew a batch of homebrew. The Underground Brewers of Connecticut have 911 meetings, which any member can call. A 911 meeting is when six to eight people get together to taste or brew beer. These meetings usually occur when a member returns from a trip with special beers. The Boreal Bottlers in Minnesota went cross-country skiing together, and numerous clubs report gathering for bicycle trips or hiking adventures.

SPECIAL EVENTS

Occasionally your club may require a booster shot of excitement. Interjecting special events into your yearly calendar will keep your members interested. Special event ideas generally fall into two categories: those arranged for club members and those involving the general public.

Events designed for members typically are of a social nature. Your club may elect to hold an annual picnic or holiday party. Such annual events provide the members something club-related to anticipate with relish. BURP recently celebrated its 10th anniversary by brewing a Thomas Hardy style ale to drink on their 20th anniversary! Several clubs hold annual Mayfest celebrations, and of course there is the ever popular and essential Oktoberfest celebration. The Boston

Wort Processors went on a beer tour of Belgium. What a great
idea for a field trip! Ask your local travel agent about group
rates on airfare and lodging; they are often available with
substantial discounts.

When preparing social events that will involve the general public try to make the event fun and educational. You
might hold a commercial beer tasting in conjunction with a
local retailer, importer, restaurant or pub. Provide the public
with a person knowledgeable in beer styles and beer flavors to
guide them on their perceptual odyssey. You might organize
a pub crawl in your area, selling tickets and providing vans
with designated drivers. Pub crawls are great ways to spend
the day with fellow brewers and others interested in the art of
brewing. You might also become involved in community
events for charity. For instance you might, as a club, participate in a walk-a-thon for charity, donate some members' time
to local efforts to combat illiteracy, or volunteer to clean up a
local park or waterway. Events for the public should provide
an opportunity to learn about beer, integrate the club into the
local community, or both.

CONCLUSION

Do you and your friends love to brew but wish that you
had a local club? With a group of creative brewers (all homebrewers have to be at least a little creative) and the suggestions given here, you and your friends can start a successful
and dynamic club. As a club you can learn more about beer
and learn faster than if you brew alone. As an organized club
you can develop a sense of pride and professionalism, as well
as contribute to your local community.

And what about brewing friends who want to liven up
their existing club? Try changing your meeting format or

adding a special event. Establish committees to accomplish goals and involve the members in planning club activities. Help create a sense of pride in the club. You may have to play cheerleader for a few months, but such enthusiasm, when presented in the context of a plan to achieve club goals, can really spice up a club.

A group of brewers can find many reasons to form a homebrew club or to liven-up an existing one. Use your own ingenuity and the processes reviewed in this paper to start your own brewclub or to raise the participation level in your existing club. Always remember that there are many other homebrewers and clubs around the world. If you run into a jam, or have a nagging problem that will not go away, call someone at another club (many phone numbers appear in *zymurgy*). The chances are that another club has already dealt with your particular problem and may have found a solution. An integrated approach to achieving goals works best. Do not forget to link up with clubs that can share their solutions with you.

Thom Tomlinson, Ph.D., manages the Great American Beer Festival's Professional Panel Blind Tasting and is president of Boulder County's homebrew club, Hop Barley & the Ale'rs. With wife Diane and a Siamese cat named Samantha, he conjures up award-winning stouts. When not involved in brewing he teaches and conducts research in psychology at the University of Colorado.

APPENDIX

HOP BARLEY AND THE ALE'RS
BY-LAWS
Approved August 24, 1989

ARTICLE I — PURPOSE

Section 1 - Purpose
To enjoy and promote the hobby of homebrewing.

Section 2 - Goals
To engage in enjoyable social activities focused on homebrewing as a common foundation.

To learn more about beer, beer tasting, beer judging and brewing techniques, based on sharing knowledge and experience.

To promote the hobby and enjoyment of homebrewing.

To promote the responsible use of alcoholic beverages.

ARTICLE II — MEMBERSHIP

Section 1 - Eligibility
All persons of legal age in the State of Colorado to consume alcoholic beverages are eligible for membership.

Section 2 - Acceptance
The only criteria for membership acceptance is to make application to the club and to keep the annual dues current.

Section 3 - Rights and Liability of Members
Each regular member of the club shall have the right to vote on club matters. Other types of members may also vote subject to the limits of Article II Section 8. The members of the club shall not be liable for the debts or obligation of the club. No member shall receive compensation for services rendered to the club except as otherwise approved by the officers of the club. A club member may be reimbursed for expenses reasonably incurred on behalf of the chapter, if approved by the club officers.

Section 4 - Guests

Members may bring guests to club meetings and fuctions. It is anticipated that these guests would eventually join the club.

Section 5 - Membership Year

The membership year of the club shall be the calendar year.

Section 6 - Non-Discrimination

Club membership shall not be denied to any individual on the basis of race, color, creed, national origin, or sex.

Section 7 - Hold Harmless

My participation in this club is entirely voluntary. I know that participation in club activities involves the consumption of an alcoholic beverage and this may affect my perception and reactions. I accept responsibility for my conduct, behavior and actions and absolve Hop, Barley and the Ale'rs of responsibility for my conduct, behavior and actions. Participation includes any guests that may be present at club activities, wherever they may be held.

Section 8 - Types of Membership

All types of membership are subject to Sections 1 and 2 of Article II.

A - Regular Members

Open to all persons as provided by Sections 1 and 2 of Article II. Dues for a regular member will be set by the officers.

B - Student Members

Open to students at an institute approved by the officers and possessing a valid student ID. Student members are not eligible to become officers. Dues for a student member will be set by the officers, at a rate less than the dues for a regular member.

C - Associate Members

Open to all who are full, or equivalent, members of any other homebrew club approved by the officers for this purpose. Approved club must have similar arrangement for full members of Hop, Barley and the Ale'rs. Associate members are not eligible to become officers. Associate members may not represent Hop, Barley and the Ale'rs in any AHA Club Competition or similar event as determined by the officers. Dues for an associate member will be set by the officers, at a rate less than the dues for a regular member.

D- Complimentary Members

The officers may offer complimentary memberships to officers of clubs approved for associate membership under Section 8C. A maximum of 5 complimentary memberships may be offered to any club. Complimentary members shall not have voting rights, and are not eligible to become officers. Complimentary members may not represent Hop, Barley and the Ale'rs in any AHA Club Competition or similar event as determined by the officers.

E - Institute Member

Officers may award institute sponsor membership to organizations or companies in exchange for services or other benefits to the club or its members. Institute members shall not have voting rights, and are not eligible to become officers.

Section 9 - Upgrading of Types of Membership

Any member may change to regular member by paying the difference in dues for the current period that dues were last paid.

ARTICLE III — VOTING

Section 1 - Eligibility

All club members, of any membership type that has voting rights (according to Article II Section 8), and who have dues paid up current are eligible to vote.

Section 2 - Items Put to Vote

The Club's officers shall decide when and the kinds of issues and topics to be voted on by the membership. Any member may petition to any officer for issues to be brought to a vote.

Section 3 - Quorum

A meeting consisting of at least one officer and one-third of the regular club members is to be considered a quorum.

Section 4 - Election Dates

Elelctions are held yearly in October with the new officers taking office in November.

Section 5 - Nominations
Nominations shall be made by the nominating committee or from any member.

Section 6 - Voting Method
Voting is by controlled ballot. This means a ballot will be available to the registered membership only.

ARTICLE IV — OFFICERS

Section 1 - Officers
The following positions make up the entirety of the club's officers:
President
Vice President
Secretary
Treasurer
Past President

Section 2 - Officer Responsibilities
President - This officer will normally conduct the meetings. He or she will be responsible for securing the meeting place. Often, the president is the one who plans the meetings, arranging for an interesting demonstration or discussion. This officer reviews the financial records of the organization quarterly or as needed.

Vice President - This person assists the president. This person will organize the tasting portion of the meeting and insure that there is an adequate supply of beer.

Secretary - This officer keeps the minutes of the meeting (if necessary), edits and publishes the club newsletter. The secretary also maintains the club membership list. The secretary also corresponds will other clubs and appropriate bodies.

Treasurer - This officer handles the finances. The treasurer collects dues and sees that they are deposited in the club's accounts. The treasurer keeps the financial records.

Past President - This officer assists the current officers as needed.

Section 3 - Removal

Any offier of the club may be removed by the vote of a majority of the members. Such a vote must be recommended by a club officer. Notification to the membership that an election will be conducted on the removal of an officer must be included in the regular notice of the monthly meeting.

Section 4 - Officer Resignation

Upon the resignation of an officer, the remaining officers shall select a person to take the responsibilities of the officer who left and this person shall serve out the remainder of the resigned officer's term.

ARTICLE V — NONPROFIT ORGANIZATION

Section 1- Nonprofit Status

The club is declared as a nonprofit organization. This does not give it tax exemption status under the rules of the United States Department of Internal Revenue Service (IRS) unless applied for and received at a later date.

ARTICLE VI — CALENDAR YEAR

Section 1 - Calendar

Dues are paid annually in January or before for the ensuing calendar year. The dues for all types of membership are set by the officers. When current members pay their dues, they must pay dues, for their type of membership, for the full year. New members are charged full dues for their level of membership if they join in the first half of the calendar year. New members will be charged one half the full dues for their type of membership if they join in the last half of the calendar year.

ARTICLE VII — DUES

Section 1 - Calendar

Dues are paid annually in January or before for the ensuing calendar year. The dues are set by the officers. When current members pay their dues, they must pay dues for the full year.

New members are charged full dues if they join in the first half of the fiscal year. Dues are one half the regular dues for new members who sign up in the last half of the fiscal year.

Section 2 - 1990 Calendar Year

Currently, the dues are paid through October 1989. The dues for 1990 will be paid in November and will include a 14-month period. This will cover the last two months of 1989 and all of 1990.

Section 3 - Form

Dues will be collected by the treasurer and may be paid in cash, money order, traveler's check, personal check and all other cash-based negotiable media.

Section 4 - Reporting

The treasurer shall report the financial status of the club at each meeting.

ARTICLE VIII — MEETINGS

Section 1 - Meetings of Members

Members shall meet monthly unless otherwise instructed by the club officers.

Section 2 - Meeting Procedure

In transacting official business, the rules of Parliamentary Procedure contained in Roberts' "Rules of Order" shall generally govern all meetings of the club.

ARTICLE IX — CONTINGENCY FUND

Section 1 - Fund

A contingency fund will be established and maintained by the treasurer to cover unexpected expenses or losses of the association. The amount of the fund shall be established by the club officers.

ARTICLE X — BY-LAW ACCEPTANCE CHANGES

Section 1 - Acceptance

These by-laws are accepted at the time of adoption by a majority vote of registered members.

Section 2 - Procedure for Changes

Any members may petition for a change in the by-laws. When changes are suggested, the petition must be presented in writing and introduced at a regular meeting of the organization. The proposed changes shall be published in the newsletter and will be voted on at the next regular club meeting provided a 30-day waiting period has been met. A vote of the majority of the club's current members that are eligible to vote according to Article II Section 8 must approve a by-law change.

9. Just Brew It—With a Wort Chiller

Jeff Frane
Vice Chairman, AHA Board of Advisers

The root question, of course, is why anyone would need a wort chiller at all. Most of us probably started homebrewing with canned malt extract, or perhaps a combination of extracts and grains. We cooled the few gallons of concentrated wort we'd boiled to pitching temperature by combining it with an equal amount of cold water and waiting many hours (anyone remember getting up at 3:00 in the morning to see if the wort was ready yet?). Or perhaps we sped up the process by submerging the brew kettle in a sink full of cold water before adding the contents to the fermenter.

There isn't any question, really, that better beer—whether all-grain or extract-based—can be made by using a full wort boil. However, rapidly cooling five or 10 gallons of boiling wort down to pitching temperature without adding cold water requires some help from the laws of physics.

Jeff Frane

Traditional brewers used devices called coolships— great shallow pans that increased the hot liquid's surface area and allowed the heat to dissipate. Coolships also exposed the wort to the air, of course, and offered no protection from airborne organisms. (That is probably just fine if you happen to live in Belgium's Payottenland; otherwise, it's likely to be a problem.) In those old breweries, "steam from the hot wort condenses on the ceiling, walls and beams of the cooler room and drips back into the wort and is a prolific cause of infection" (de Clerck, 1957, p. 341). Systems like this also required an extended plant to recover wort from the sludge at the bottom of the cooling pan. Later, breweries added refrigeration units, which eventually supplanted the coolship entirely. Today, a few breweries still use coolships, but most use a form of heat exchange cooler in which cold water absorbs the heat from the wort as the two liquids pass on either side of a metal barrier. After the wort has been cooled, sterile oxygen is injected to ensure a vigorous fermentation. The same principles of heat exchange used in a commercial brewery can be applied at home through the use of a wort chiller.

HOT BREAK/COLD BREAK

In addition to bringing the wort to fermentation temperature as soon as possible, rapid cooling also causes changes in the wort that encourage good fermentation and brighter beer. At two late stages in the boiling/cooling cycle, there is an opportunity to clear the proteins, hop resins and other organic matter that would discourage healthy yeast growth and cloud the finished beer.

The hot break occurs while the wort is still in the kettle and is, in fact, considered to be the right time to end the boil. It is marked by the appearance of large flakes of "gunk" surrounded by a brilliantly clear wort. The cold break—which consists of similar organic compounds—begins after the wort has been cooled below 60 degrees C (140 degrees F). George Fix writes that "by removing most of both precipitates, one can eliminate approximately one-half of the haze-forming material" (Fix, 1989, p. 121). While it is essential in the making of fine beer to ensure a proper hot break and to rack the wort off the precipitate, some homebrewers are overly cautious about "protecting" their beer from the cold break.

After touring through a few microbreweries, it is clear to me that cold break sediment is not nearly as threatening as it seems at first glance; the most common systems create a cold break but do nothing to eliminate it. Consider Jean de Clerck's statement: "It is therefore essential, that while the sterility of the wort is assured, it should (1) absorb sufficient oxygen during cooling, (2) coagulated protein should be entirely eliminated, and (3) the turbid matter *which appears during cooling should be at least partly precipitated, so that it does not remain as a fine colloidal suspension in the beer*" (emphasis added) (1957, p. 333). In other words, what is essential is ensuring the cold break; once precipitated out, the material will only cause problems if it is redissolved by raising the temperature again.

George Fix writes that "in preparing my book on brewing science I tried to carefully study the effects of cold break carryover, and found that as far as finished beer flavors were concerned there were none" (Fix, 1992). In that book (*Principles of Brewing Science*), in fact, Fix explains that in adverse conditions such as a shortage of oxygen, the trub can be utilized in yeast metabolism (Fix, 1989). He cautions that bacteria can use trub in the same way, but "if bacterial levels are sufficiently low both in the chilled wort and in the pitching yeast, then I believe there will be no problems from cold break carryover" (Fix, 1992). With proper sanitation, then, and the use of pure cultured brewing yeast, the carryover from cold break should not prove a problem to the homebrewer.

IMMERSION VS. COUNTERFLOW . . . AND BEYOND

Having decided to build a wort chiller, the homebrewer is faced with two main choices: immersion or counterflow. In both cases, cold water runs through a metal (usually copper) tube and absorbs the heat from the wort. In an immersion chiller, the coil of tubing is plunged directly into the kettle and the wort is transferred to the fermenter after it has been cooled. The counterflow chiller cools the wort as it is traveling out of the kettle, so that it arrives in the fermenter at the correct temperature. As with most choices facing the homebrewer (liquid vs. dry yeast, pelletized vs. loose hops, extract vs. all grains), each has its apparent advantages and problems, and each has its partisans.

Partisans of the immersion chiller present a very good argument. First of all, the basic unit is extremely simple and inexpensive to produce, requiring only 30 to 50 feet of copper tubing, and some simple fittings to adapt the tubing to common garden connections. Second, an immersion chiller requires no effort to sanitize: simply plunge the clean chiller into the boiling wort for 15 minutes before ending the boil. (Caution must be taken, however, that there is no water in the chiller when it is placed in the boiling wort; any liquid will be heated to steam and will blast out of the chiller.)

A counterflow chiller, by contrast, requires some time to construct (although we shall see that it isn't much time, and components are likewise quite inexpensive). It also requires some effort to sanitize, although not as much as some brewers seem to fear. Furthermore, it is generally faster than an immersion chiller, dropping wort temperature from boiling to a safe pitching level in the amount of time it takes to siphon the wort into a fermenter.

Perhaps most importantly, with a counterflow system, the wort is protected from the environment during a critical time. As de Clerck notes: "The most dangerous period from this standpoint is when the wort is being cooled from 40 degrees to 20 degrees C [104 to 68 degrees F] which is the most favorable temperature range for bacterial development. . . . On grounds of hygiene, it is preferable to cool the wort in enclosed coolers"(1957, p. 333). Brewers using an immersion chiller need to be particularly careful to protect the wort in the kettle once its temperature drops into this critical range.

By contrast, the immersion chiller gradually brings the wort down through the temperature range—in what is most likely an open container. Further, most immersion chillers are not efficient enough to rapidly cool the wort without periodic (or even constant) agitation—another potential source of contamination, and a possible source of wort oxidation if the agitation occurs while the wort is still hot.

One of the perceived advantages of an immersion chiller is that it leaves both the hot and cold breaks behind in the kettle. But if the transfer of cold break material into the fermenter is, in fact, not a problem, then this advantage loses significance.

BASIC DESIGNS—AND VARIATIONS

One of the things that continues to amaze me about homebrewers is how ingenious they are. When I started to research this presentation, I circulated a short questionnaire among the homebrewers on Internet, a worldwide computer network. I asked people whether they preferred immersion or counterflow wort chillers and why. I received about 40 replies, not only addressing my questions but offering an array of design suggestions and problem resolutions. As I've come to expect from homebrewers, the suggestions were frequently incisive and inventive. There also were lively discussions during the three presentations I made at the conference in Milwaukee; several of the excellent suggestions made have been incorporated here.

The simplest immersion chiller consists of 30 to 50 feet of 3/8- or 1/2-inch copper tubing with a fitting at each end to accept a garden hose (see Figure 1). Cold tap water runs in one end, courses through the tubing and emerges—hot—on the other end. Some of the Internet brewers, however, found this design to not be completely effective. Alan Edwards of Modesto, California, wound his 50 feet of tubing into three separate coils and added a "pre-chiller coil" of about 10 feet

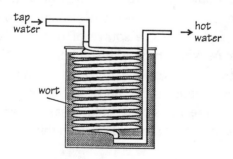

Figure 1. Simple immersion chiller.

that is immersed in a sink of ice water to drop the water temperature well below that available from the tap (see Figure 2). He cautions, "If you try this, be careful when you coil the inside set . . . it's easy to kink the copper if you try to coil it too tightly."

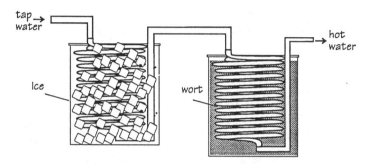

Figure 2. Immersion chiller with ice pre-cooling coil.

Geoff Sherwood has built was he calls a "mongo immersion chiller," and it really is that. "It has 100 feet of 3/8 copper set up into two independent coils fed by a T fitting on inlet and collected by a T fitting on outlet." He found that it was necessary to put the two coils in parallel (rather than series) because of the resistance of the 100-foot length. Geoff reported that he is able to cool 10 gallons of boiling wort to 72 degrees F (22 degrees C) in eight minutes.

Alan's system of pre-chilling is actually a pretty common response to the limitations of the basic immersion chiller. But San Francisco's Russ Wigglesworth described one of the more bizarre variations. He has 50 feet of 3/8-inch copper "coiled in a 9-gallon tub. The tube connects to the spigot on my kettle and drains into a carboy via a sanitized hose at the exit end. I also have a 30-quart ice chest in which I put an immersible pump. The 9-gallon tub has a drain which allows it to empty into the ice chest. I fill the 9-gallon tub with water and the ice chest with ice and enough water to prime the pump. This circulates the ice water and increases the heat transfer like a counter flow without the waste of water. I freeze my own blocks of ice in plastic containers and reclaim the water from the chiller as it warms and requires additional blocks of ice." Although Russ is aware of problems with his system, he finds it has great advantages in an area where water conservation is a major issue.

Counterflow chillers are of two basic styles. A very simple system can be built by coiling copper tubing within a PVC pipe, which is then capped, with hose fittings added to either end. The copper tubing passes out either through the caps or through the wall of the tube. The system doesn't allow for a great length of copper tubing to be used (unless the PVC pipe is very long) (see Figure 3).

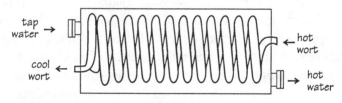

Figure 3. Canister-type counterflow chiller.

The more common design, and the one I will describe how to build, simply runs 25 feet of 3/8-inch copper tubing down a length of garden hose. The unit is coiled to conserve space. Hot wort runs down the copper tubing while cold tap water flows the opposite direction through the garden hose. Hot water emerges from the opposite end of the garden hose and cool wort from the far end of the copper tubing. With no seams in the copper tubing, the chiller is easy to sanitize.

WORT CHILLER CONSTRUCTION

As a totally un-handy sort of brewer, I am indebted to my old brewing partner, Pete Jelinek, for producing this wort chiller design. One of the great advantages of the design is that it does not require any welding or soldering—given my "skills" at torch-welding, this is an absolute necessity! The parts list is as follows:

2 galvanized "T"s, 1/2-inch
2 compression fittings, 1/2 inch mpt x 3/8 inch
2 hose barb fittings, 1/2 inch
2 garden hose fittings ("double male hose-to-pipe nipple"—1/2 inch NPT x 3/4 inch GHT)
25 feet of 3/8-inch copper tubing
24 feet of garden hose (no connections)
2 hose clamps
wire or tie wraps

All of these parts should be available at a good hardware store. The copper tubing is soft and is used primarily in refrigeration units. As it turned out, I found all the other metal parts except the "T" in brass. The tricky bits are the compression fitting and the hose barb. The latter must be selected carefully, and there are a lot of variations. The threaded end obviously must be 1/2 inch, but the barb must have a very thin wall to hold the garden hose and allow the 3/8-inch copper tubing to fit loosely. The first hose barb I bought, which was supposedly 1/2 x 1/2 inch, fit so snugly on the tubing that no water would be able to flow around it. During the presentations in Milwaukee, it was pointed out to me that one solution would be to use a hose and hose barb with a larger o.d.; however, a brewer whose club built a chiller along those lines said that it did not work well. Another suggestion, obvious in retrospect, called for adding regular garden fittings to the hose, and using a second male hose-to-pipe nipple so that the garden hose can simply be screwed onto the "T".

Compression fittings come in two variations. Ideally, you should find one that allows the tubing to pass completely through it. I was assured in Milwaukee that any good plumbing supply store should have such fittings. However, some versions of this fitting have a "stop" that prevents the tubing from going through. Fortunately, brass is very soft and if this is the only sort you can find, you can use a hand drill with a 3/8-inch bit to bore out the stop.

You can look for bulk garden hose, without any fittings, but the best deal I was able to find was 50 feet of 1/2-inch garden hose for $6.99. That's hard to beat, and you can make two wort chillers out of it. I simply cut off one of the hose connectors and measured out the length I needed. You should also pick up some TFE Pipe Thread Tape with Teflon, which is a non-toxic sealant for the threaded joints.

To begin with, carefully straighten the copper tubing. The simplest way to do this is to have someone hold one end down and stretch it out on the floor. Be careful not to kink it. Then slide the hose over the tubing. You can then wrap the entire affair around a five-gallon bucket; the garden hose will help prevent any kinks forming in the copper. Put the hose clamps loosely onto the garden hose, assemble the fittings and Presto! a wort chiller.

Figure 4 shows how to construct the two end-fittings. Assemble the pieces loosely at first. The copper tubing runs through the garden hose and then through the cross-bar of the "T". To do this, it first passes through the hose barb then out through the compression fitting. This is true on both ends of

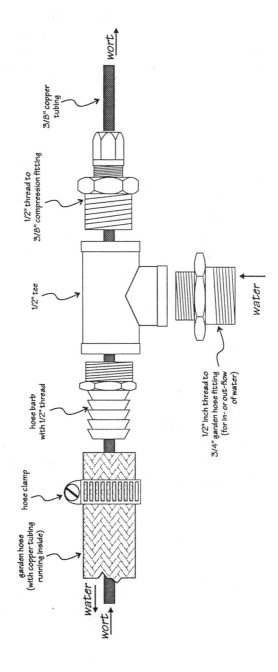

Figure 4. Detail of counterflow end fitting.

the chiller. There should be enough copper tubing projecting from either end of the chiller to attach plastic tubing. One end will connect to the kettle by some means (either to a siphon or to a tap on the bottom of the kettle) and the other will drain into the fermenter. The third entrance to the "T" will step up to a hose fitting so that you can run water into the chiller from a hose bib or laundry tub. On the other end, of course, the same fitting allows the water to flow out, either into a drain or into some kind of recovery vessel (the hot water is great for cleaning).

After everything is put together, tighten up all the fittings and you're done! Use either wire or some plastic tie wraps to bind the coils of the wort chiller together. Try running some water through the system as though it were wort, and run some water through the hose to check for leaks.

USING THE WORT CHILLER

For me the trickiest part of using a wort chiller was getting the wort into it! Eventually I arrived at a system that has worked very well, with minimal clogging. I wrapped a length of 3/8-inch copper tubing once around the outside of my kettle, with enough tubing left over to reach the top. Then I tightened the coil enough to fit on the inner perimeter of the kettle. On the bottom of the coil I drilled scores of holes with the smallest bit I could find (I used a Dremel Mototool hobby drill, so the holes are really small). This connects to the wort chiller with 3/8-inch plastic tubing.

I sanitize my fermenter (a glass carboy) with chlorine solution, and then siphon the entire amount through the clean wort chiller. This requires a separate piece of copper since the kettle coil obviously won't fit in the neck of the carboy. The easiest way to start a siphon as long as this is to back-fill the chiller with water from the tap until no air is bubbling up in the carboy. Then the siphon will start itself.

Just before the boil ends, I put the kettle coil into the kettle to sanitize it. At the end of the boil, I use a spoon to carefully start a whirlpool, then let it rest for 20 minutes or so. At the end of that time, the wort has become brilliantly clear. As the level of wort in the kettle drops, a mound of green particulate matter slowly becomes visible, like a slow-motion film of a volcano emerging from the sea. Since I use pelletized hops almost exclusively, this mound stays in the kettle and virtually every drop of wort gets into the wort chiller and into the fermenter.

I monitor the temperature as it leaves the chiller with a sanitized thermometer, controlling the flow of water until a stable pitching temperature is reached. I have a plastic ball valve (from the gardening section of the hardware store), which allows me to control flow more precisely than with the tap handle. Portland water is really cold, so very little water is necessary.

When done brewing, flush the wort chiller thoroughly. Once again, good suggestions came out of the discussion in Milwaukee. Some brewers flush their systems with TSP. Some cautioned that the flushing should run in the opposite direction from the normal flow of wort. One important point was made that the connection between the copper tubing and the plastic tubing (either down to the carboy or up to the kettle) was a potential source of infection. The plastic tubing should be removed each time the chiller is used so it can be cleaned separately.

Given all the benefits of wort chillers, and given how simple they are to build—what are you waiting for? Get out there and Brew It!

Jeff Frane is a Portland, Oregon, homebrewer and part-time writer. A member of the AHA Board of Advisers, he has been active in the local homebrewing scene for several years, running the Oregon State Fair brewing competition, teaching homebrewing, and indulging in the joys of living in Munich-on-the-Willamette. He is currently writing a simple introduction to all-grain brewing.

REFERENCES

de Clerck, J. (1957). *A Textbook of Brewing, Vol. 1.* London: Chapman & Hall.

Fix, G. (1989). *Principles of Brewing Science.* Boulder, Colo.: Brewers Publications.

Fix, G. (March 1992). Private correspondence.

13. Beer Filtration for Homebrewers

Steve Daniel
League City, Texas

I know what you are thinking right now. "Filter my homebrew? Are you nuts?!" Filtering is tantamount to beer blasphemy to the majority of homebrewers. Most folks think that filtering their beer will remove its complexity and body, and that filtration is expensive, messy and a hassle. Not only that, most brewers believe that their beer will clear up sooner or later anyway, so filtering it will not make any difference in the long run. All of these beliefs may be true to a certain extent, but I hope to demonstrate the ways in which they are inaccurate. I will explain how filtration can produce a beer with superior stability and flavor when compared with most unfiltered beers, and how it can be done cheaply, neatly and easily.

Steve Daniel

WHY FILTER?

The obvious reason to filter beer is to make it clear and bright in less time than it would take to become that way naturally, but this is not the only benefit a filtered beer receives. After fermentation has ceased, most homebrewers allow their beer to settle and clarify before conditioning it. During this settling process the beer is left wide open to contamination by undesirable wild yeasts, which, if left unchecked, will produce a second fermentation.

This is especially true when commercially prepared dried yeast is used, because it is nearly always contaminated to some degree with wild yeast. The wild yeast may be in the beer from the beginning of fermentation, but it is usually overwhelmed by the "good" yeast during the initial fermentation. However, it is more than willing to wait patiently until that yeast consumes all the simple sugars and begins to settle out. The wild yeast will then propagate and begin to ferment the more complex sugars that have not been consumed by the somewhat finicky "good" yeast.

Wild yeast produces not only the usual ethanol and carbon dioxide, but also complex alcohols such as phenol, which imparts a clovelike flavor to the finished beer. While this characteristic may be desirable in a German wheat beer or a Belgian ale, it is not at all appropriate for most other beer styles. Wild yeast's consumption of the more complex, body-building sugars also results in a more alcoholic beer that may taste watered-down and unbalanced.

If the beer is bottled or kegged prior to the onset of a second fermentation, this fermentation may be delayed, but it will occur eventually. The only difference is that it will take place in the keg or bottle rather than in the secondary fermenter. During the conditioning process the wild yeast will continue to consume complex sugars and produce carbon dioxide long after the good yeast has done its job. This may result in "gushers" or even "beer bombs" caused by severe over-carbonation after several months of conditioning. Fortunately for the homebrewer, filtration can eliminate these wild yeast problems. If handled properly, the beer can usually be made ready for filtration in as little as a week after fermentation is complete. Filtration at this time will result in the removal of the wild yeast and will therefore prevent the second fermentation from taking place.

Another benefit received by removing the yeast is that the formation of other undesirable flavors such as yeast bite is prevented. Like any living organism, yeast needs food to survive. When the yeast normally left in our beer runs out of food it dies and begins to decompose. This is what is known in beer nomenclature as yeast autolysis. The flavor produced by the rotting yeast has been compared to spoiled fruit and vegetables, and even to wet cardboard. In heavier beers this flavor may be completely masked by the generous use of hops and malt, but it will hang over more delicate beer styles like a cheap (and smelly) suit. Obviously, removing the yeast by filtration before autolysis begins will prevent the occurrence of this process and will allow the beer to be stored for long periods of time without significant degradation of its flavor.

In my opinion, the most important reason to filter beer is that it will be ready to drink much sooner than if clarification

The Lakefront Brewery of Milwaukee, at the outdoor festival on the last day of the conference.

is left to happen on its own. After a beer has been racked to the secondary fermenter and allowed to settle, it may take three or four weeks to clear up before it is ready to be bottled or kegged. If the beer is refrigerated in the secondary, proteins will begin to join together and form a haze in the beer which can take months of lagering to get rid of. If the beer is kept very cold for about a week before it is filtered, nearly all of the haze forming proteins will be removed when it is filtered. The result is a brilliantly clear beer which can be ready for consumption in as little as a third of the time it would take for it to clear on its own.

As you can clearly see, filtering beer does more than simply make it look pretty. It results in a stable product that will not gush, and will not taste thinner, phenolic, or yeast bitten when a bottle is opened or a keg is tapped a few months down the road. Not only that, it will not be necessary to wait nearly as long to enjoy it!

SO WHAT'S THE CATCH?

There is really only one catch—it is necessary to use soda kegs or another suitable system that will allow pressurized transfer of five-gallon batches of beer from one sealed container to another. Because this paper is geared toward intermediate brewers, most of you have already started using soda kegs, or are planning to in the near future, so this should not be a major problem. Transferring the brilliantly clear filtered beer from the keg into bottles as the need arises is no great obstacle either, now that counter-pressure bottle fillers are widely available for a reasonable price (about $20).

SHOULD ALL BEER BE FILTERED?

As you can probably guess, the answer to this question is an emphatic no! Some beers rely heavily on long periods of bottle maturation to enhance their complexity, and the yeast plays no small role in the beer's development. As the beer ages, the flavor compounds produced by the decaying yeast blend with other flavors already present to produce still more complex and interesting characteristics. Most Belgian ales are aged for many months or even years at the brewery before they are ready for consumption. Barley wines such as Thomas Hardy's Ale may require laying down for a minimum of five years before the full complexity of their flavor begins to unfold, and they will continue to improve for 25 years or longer (if you can manage to wait that long!). These and other traditionally bottle-conditioned beer styles are especially suited to long maturation periods—either because of their acidic qualities, as is the case with Belgian ales, or through the generous use of hops and malt, as with barley wines. These are certainly not the only beer styles that fare better when they are left on the yeast, but they provide good examples for this discussion.

Lighter beer styles that are not as "yeast friendly" as Belgian ales or barley wines do not hold up nearly as well over long periods of time, and are actually at their peak the day they leave the brewery. It therefore behooves homebrewers to get their lighter beers ready for consumption as soon as possible, so they will have longer to enjoy them before they begin to "go south." Most pale and amber lagers, including American light, Continental light, Oktoberfest, California common beer, as well as medium-bodied light and amber ales, are excellent candidates for filtration. You may be surprised that I would recommend filtering a pale ale, but this is not an uncommon practice in breweries in England or the United States. Sierra Nevada Brewing Co. filters its bottled products because this practice significantly increases the beer's shelf life. Some dark beer styles such as Munich dunkel and alt also can be filtered with excellent results. I have even filtered a traditional German bock with great success, though I will leave it up to you to determine whether heavier styles such as this are suitable for filtration.

WHAT POROSITY WORKS BEST?

If too fine a filter is used, some body and color may be stripped from the finished product, rendering it noticeably thinner and less interesting. On the other hand, if the filter is overly coarse it will not remove all of the bad stuff we are trying to get rid of in the first place. As with most of life's dilemmas, a happy medium can be reached somewhere between doing nothing at all and doing too much to the beer. It is possible to choose a filter with a porosity that will produce a brilliantly clear beer and not remove a significant amount of the body and complexity from the finished product in the process. I have found that a filter rated at 0.5 microns is the best all-around size to use. From my observations, it will remove all the yeast as well as large proteins from the beer. I have not noticed any reduction of flavor or body using my particular 0.5 micron unit, though some people may dispute this observation.

Pore size is not the only concern when it comes to choosing a filter. A filter's efficiency, which may be expressed in percent or beta units, is based on how well it can trap smaller particles. A 0.5 micron filter with a 90 percent efficiency rating will allow 10 percent of particles 0.5 microns in size to pass through. The same filter would be rated at 10 beta units because 10 0.5 micron particles must enter the filter for one particle to pass completely through. The best filters are usually rated at 99 percent efficiency or greater, which is equivalent to 100 beta units. The 0.5 micron filter I am presently using is rated at 99.9 percent efficiency.

WHAT KIND OF FILTER IS BEST TO BUY?

If I am worth my salt, you should be ready to run out and plunk down some hard-earned money for a fancy new filter system right about now, but before you do, I want to relate some of my experiences with the various methods available for filtering beer. I have accidentally "bruised" my fair share of perfectly good beer by using inadequate equipment or faulty filtering techniques, and it is my hope that you will learn from my mistakes. I would also like to review the types and brands of filtration set-ups available to the average (frugal) homebrewer, so you can make a more informed decision when it comes time to buy one.

There are two basic ways to filter beer. The first—and by far the most common—way is to simply force the beer straight through the filter using carbon dioxide for pressure. The problem with this method is that the pores of the filter eventually become clogged with solid material and the pressure must be increased to keep the flow going. If too great a pressure is used, the solid material may be forced through the filter into the finished beer or, worse yet, the filter may rupture. One way to avoid this problem is to use a filter with a surface area large enough to trap all the solid material before it clogs. Fortunately, if the proper equipment is used, it will be possible to filter several five-gallon batches through a simple system without a hitch, provided a few steps are taken to prepare the beer before it is filtered (more on this later).

The other method of filtration is relatively new, and is known as tangential flow. Though it is a little more complex, it eliminates most of the clogging problems associated with conventional filtration. In tangential flow systems the beer may follow two different routes. It can either pass through the filter into the finished beer tank, or recirculate back into the primary tank through a return line. The flow of the beer into the filter is directed so that it continuously washes solids from the surface of the filter pads. These solids are carried away by the recirculating beer. This type of design results in a greatly increased filtering capacity compared to the conventional type of filter. Unfortunately, no tangential flow systems are available that are both affordable and practical for homebrewers, so we will have to make do with the conventional systems.

The two types of conventional filtration systems readily available to homebrewers are plate filters and cartridge filters.

I will discuss the advantages and disadvantages associated with each.

Plate, or Pad-Type, Filters

These filters consist of fiber filter pads pressed between grooved plastic plates. The plates act as a support for the filter pads, and the grooves in the plates facilitate the flow of beer through the filter. Some plate filters are expandable, which means that additional plates can be added to increase the filter's capacity. The filter pads can be used only once, and are usually $3 or $4 a set. This means that in addition to the initial cost of the filter, it will be necessary to pay a little extra every time the filter is used. Because the pads are typically made from a cellulose material, the filter must be assembled and flushed with water to rinse any cardboard flavors from the pads. From my experience, no matter how much I flush the filter, the first quart or so of beer filtered through one of these units always tastes like I am chewing on a shoe box. Plate filters do an excellent job of removing chill haze, but they also tend to strip a little too much body from the beer for my liking. One thing I find particularly annoying about these units is that they all leak, though I must admit the better ones are less prone to do so. There are several brands of plate filters available, and some are much better suited for our purposes than others.

Some homebrewers have had success using Vin Brite filtration systems. They are available at most homebrew stores and are relatively inexpensive, at about $30. They come with only two plastic filter plates and cannot be expanded. A filter pad is placed on each plate and the assembly is clamped shut with bolts and wing nuts. This system is great for filtering wine, but as you might guess, there is a big difference between filtering wine and beer. Typically, wine is nearly free of solid matter when it is filtered, and can easily be pushed through the system with a minimal amount of pressure. Beer is not nearly as clear to start out with, and may require the addition of as much as 20 pounds of pressure to facilitate filtration. This may not sound like a lot, but it adds up to nearly 2,000 pounds of total force being exerted outward on each plastic plate, which is more than enough to cause them to rupture. Homebrewers have resorted to rigging up steel bars and clamps to reinforce the filter plates, but the unit is still prone to leak excessively and is generally more trouble than it is worth for this application.

There are some higher quality pad systems worthy of consideration by homebrewers. Marcon, a Canadian manufacturer, has filter systems to suit the needs of everyone from homebrewers to large-scale brewpub operators. Their systems, which employ the use of reinforced plates and metal frames, are very well designed and are specifically made to filter beer under pressure. A big advantage of these systems is that extra filter plates can be added as necessary to satisfy any increase in filtering requirements. The biggest drawback of the Marcon units is their price. The bottom-of-the-line system runs around $200, which puts it out of reach for most of us. However, if you can afford it, these are definitely the Cadillacs of filtration systems.

Cartridge Filters

These systems are very common and are widely used as under-the-sink water filters in homes. They are designed for high pressure applications and can be modified to filter beer by simply adding a one-quarter-inch hose barb to the filter's inlet and outlet. Cartridge filters consist of a cylindrical plastic housing into which a filter cartridge is inserted. The housing is sealed with a lid and an o-ring, which makes the filter practically leak-free. Some filter housings are available in clear plastic, which makes it possible to observe the beer as it is being filtered. I have not figured out any advantage to a clear housing, and in my opinion it is more of a novelty than a useful feature. The most outstanding qualities of cartridge filters is what they cost now and what they cost later. A top-quality set-up can be purchased for about $60, and the filter cartridges are reusable indefinitely. They are usually made of an inert plastic such as polypropylene, which means they will not impart any unpleasant flavors to the finished product. After they are used, the cartridges can be soaked in a mild caustic solution to break down the organic matter trapped inside them. They can then be flushed with clean water and stored until they are needed for the next batch. I have used the same cartridge to filter several hundred gallons of beer over the last couple of years, and it is still going strong. If I could recommend one type of filter system for all homebrewers, a cartridge system would easily be my first choice. But please beware! There are two basic types of filter cartridges available for this kind of system, and there is a world of difference between them.

Spun cartridges, which resemble a spool of twine, are made by wrapping a fibrous "string" around a hollow perforated tube. These cartridges are very cheap, and in this case you get what you pay for. Because they are relatively thick, any material imbedded within them is difficult to flush out, which makes it hard to clean them thoroughly. They have a tendency to clog, and may allow some solid material to pass through. They usually lack gaskets on the ends of the cartridge, which can make it very difficult to obtain a good seal against the filter housing. In other words, a beer can be passed through a spun cartridge and still come out cloudy because a faulty seal allowed beer to go around the filter instead of through it. I have had nothing but trouble with spun cartridges, and therefore suggest avoiding them under any circumstances.

Pleated cartridges are considerably more expensive, and are worth twice the price. They consist of a sheet of highly efficient filter fabric folded in an accordion-like fashion and wrapped around a perforated support tube. The cartridge is surrounded by a protective mesh cylinder and is sealed on both ends. The filter fabric used in these cartridges is strong and thin, which makes them easy to clean. Any material trapped in the fabric can be flushed out of the filter readily once it has been soaked in caustic. Most pleated cartridges come with built-in gaskets, which will ensure a proper seal against the housing every time. Generally speaking, pleated cartridges are very dependable and will last a long time if they are properly cared for. As you can probably guess by now, this is the type of cartridge I recommend.

Who Has Pleated Cartridges?

Most stores carry only 5 micron and larger sizes of spun cartridges, which are intended for use as water filters. It probably will be necessary to contact a store that specializes in filters to get high quality pleated units. I have done business with The Filter Store located in Rush, New York, and have found the people there to be knowledgeable, friendly and helpful. They sell a Home Brewing Filtration Kit which I consider to be one of the best filter values on the market. The kit is of very high quality, consisting of a clear plastic filter housing and a 0.5 micron pleated polypropylene filter cartridge rated at 99.9 percent efficiency. It comes complete with all the hoses and fittings needed to filter beer (except for a couple of soda keg connectors), and is a steal at about $60. This is the same system I have been using for the past two years. It has produced crystal clear beer every time I have used it, and I couldn't be happier with its performance. Anyone interested in contacting The Filter Store can obtain more information from one of their advertisements in a current issue of *zymurgy*.

IS THERE ANYTHING ELSE?

Finally, I will offer a few tips on how to get started filtering beer.

1. In order to remove chill haze, cool the beer to close to 32 degrees F (0 degrees C) and keep it there for about a week prior to filtration. During this time the proteins in the beer will fall out of solution and join together to form macromolecules larger than 0.5 microns. After the large proteins have formed, the beer can be filtered and the chill haze will be removed along with the yeast. If sufficient time is not allowed for the proteins to join, they will simply pass through the filter, and the beer will remain cloudy. I have determined through trial and error that one week is the minimum amount of refrigeration time required.

2. It is best to filter flat, or nearly flat beer. If conditioned beer is filtered it will tend to foam, which slows down the process considerably. If necessary, a small amount of counterpressure can be used in the finished beer tank to reduce foaming. The flat beer should be force-carbonated immediately after filtration and will be ready to drink the next day.

3. Never use chlorine bleach to clean a pleated cartridge! Chlorine will break down the filter fabric and degrade its performance over a period of time. Use B-Brite or a similar

commercial preparation to sanitize the filter before each use. Mix the sanitizing solution in a soda canister and use carbon dioxide pressure to pump it through the filter. When the filter and transfer lines are full of solution, allow them to stand for 15 minutes before flushing. Fill the canister with five gallons of cold water and flush the filter to remove all traces of the solution. When the canister of water blows empty, invert the filter assembly to purge the remaining water from it. The filter is now ready to use.

New filters should be soaked in a mild baking soda solution or in beer for a few days before they are used. This will condition them and remove any off-flavors that may be present in the new filter fabric.

4. Never exceed 20 pounds per square inch of pressure when filtering. Greater pressures may cause the pleated cartridge to fail. The filter housings are usually rated at over 100 pounds per square inch, so there is no chance that they will rupture under normal use.

5. Soak the filter in a 1 percent caustic solution for a day or so after each use. Reassemble the filter unit and pump cold tap water through the filter to flush out the caustic solution. Place the filter in a large Zip-Loc bag with enough water to keep it wet, and store it in the refrigerator to keep it from getting moldy. It is important to keep the filter wet between uses; otherwise, it will not work at peak efficiency.

That's all there is to it. I hope your filtering system will give you as much satisfaction as mine has provided for me. I am sure that once you see and taste the results, you will be convinced that filtration is definitely worth the extra effort. Good luck!

Steve Daniel, known by his friends as "Negative Man," has been brewing for nearly 10 years. He is a long-distance member of The Boston Wort Processors, and likes to brew German-style beers with his wife Christina when he is not working as an industrial hygienist for a major chemical company. He hopes to open his own brewpub someday, but until then he will have to be satisfied with making an occasional batch of pretty tasty light lager.

11. Oxygen: Friend or Foe?

Alberta Rager
BJCP National Beer Judge

Oxygen is like a double edged sword—it is a necessity for healthy vigorous yeast growth and development, but, if introduced to hot wort or after respiration, it can have a deleterious effect on the finished beer.

YEAST PREPARATION AND RESPIRATION

The initial period in the life cycle of yeast is one of preparation and respiration. During the preparation phase, the yeast first prepares the cell walls while taking on nitrogen, sugar and oxygen. Once the wort sugars and nitrogen enter the cell, the yeast begins to respire.

During respiration, the yeast stores energy derived from the sugar and oxygen for the remainder of its life cycle. A crucial element during respiration is "free oxygen"—oxygen

Alberta Rager

that is dissolved in the beer wort. Therefore, wort respiration is referred to as an aerobic process. At this point dissolved oxygen can be considered a yeast nutrient. The uptake of dissolved oxygen occurs rather quickly, usually within a few hours. The yeast consumes all the oxygen that the wort contains as it synthesizes sterols. During respiration the yeast reproduces while producing carbon dioxide, water and beer flavors. No alcohol is being produced at this point. The availability of oxygen will determine when fermentation begins and ends. During respiration there is no disadvantage to having too much oxygen in your wort. Once a strong, vigorous yeast growth has saturated the wort, fermentation will begin.

WHEN AND HOW TO INJECT OXYGEN

During the wort boil the dissolved oxygen will leave solution and volitize in the steam vapors. This means that the free oxygen required during respiration must be introduced following the boil, after the wort is cool. Introducing oxygen to the wort while it is still hot greatly increases the level of oxidation and other undesirable fermentation byproducts while leaving less oxygen available for the yeast to use during the aerobic reproductive phase. To maximize yeast yield, the cool wort should be 25 to 50 percent saturated with oxygen prior to yeast pitching.

Oxygen can be dissolved in the cooled wort by aeration or oxygenation. Aeration can be accomplished by splashing or agitating the cooled wort as it is transferred to the fermenter prior to pitching the yeast. Capping the carboy and shaking or rolling it vigorously is also effective.

Aeration can also be achieved by using an aquarium aerator with a .2 micron filter and an aquarium aeration stone attached to the outlet hose. A .2 micron filter is small enough to remove the potentially dangerous airborne bacteria and contaminants. As with all paraphernalia that comes in contact with the cooled wort, the hose and stone should be sanitized. The yeast may or may not be pitched prior to beginning aeration. The filter should be positioned in the hose so that it does not come in contact with the cooled wort. The aeration should last at least two and a half hours, but not more than 24 hours after the yeast has been pitched. The ratio of healthy, active yeast cells to the wort volume will help in determining the aeration requirement, as will wort temperature, pH, and the availability of nutrients.

Oxygenation with pure oxygen is not recommended in the homebrew environment due to the danger of fire.

RESULTS OF INSUFFICIENT OXYGEN

There are several negative consequences of insufficient aeration of the cooled wort. One is that it will often result in increased lag time. Lag time is that period after the yeast has been pitched, but prior to visible signs of fermentation. This is the period when the wort is most vulnerable to bacterial contamination, as the yeast and its competitors vie to become the strongest population. Homebrewers try to reduce the lag time by creating an environment conducive to rapid yeast growth.

Insufficient oxygen in the wort also can cause yeast degeneration, because the yeast is not able to reproduce normally under these conditions. When the oxygen supply is depleted and yeast activity switches from aerobic to anaerobic, respiration ends and fermentation begins. If there is too little oxygen dissolved in the wort during the aerobic, respiratory phase, fermentation will begin before sufficient yeast growth has occurred, and a sluggish, stuck or incomplete fermentation can result.

These problems can be avoided by aerating the wort prior to pitching or within the first 24 hours after pitching. Introducing oxygen more than 24 hours after pitching is usually deleterious.

OXYGEN AND FERMENTATION

The dissolved oxygen in the wort that is not used during the respiration cycle is driven off by carbon dioxide during fermentation as alcohol and beer flavors are being produced. Introducing oxygen during fermentation is undesirable. Bacteria may be introduced along with the oxygen, causing contamination, and undesirable oxidation characteristics are likely to result as well. Therefore, care should be exercised in preventing oxygen from contacting the fermenting wort. This can be accomplished by fermenting under closed conditions using either a blow-by or an oversized fermenter.

If using a blow-by system, sanitize a drilled stopper and siphon hose that has been placed through the hole in the stopper. Place the stopper in the opening of the carboy and the end of the hose in a container (milk jug, bucket, jar, etc.) of chlorine solution. For the first two to three days of fermentation, the blow-by will direct the overflow of fermenting foam into the awaiting container. This foam contains hops resins and yeast that can cause excessive bitterness in the finished beer. Change the chlorine solution in the container as needed to maintain a clear solution.

When the activity subsides, usually after about three days, replace the blow-by with a fermentation lock half filled with water. The lock serves as a one-way valve allowing the carbon dioxide produced during fermentation to escape while preventing oxygen and airborne bacteria from contaminating the fermenting beer.

An oversized fermenter can be a carboy which is a gallon or so larger than the volume of wort or one of many plastic single-stage fermenting buckets obtainable at your local home-brew supply shop. Fit the opening of your fermenting vessel with a sanitized drilled stopper and half-filled fermentation lock. During the active fermentation cycle, foam will rise, along with hop resins and yeast. As the fermentation slows and the foam falls, the hop resins and yeast will cling to the side and/or shoulders of the fermenting vessel.

In a closed fermentation system, the oxygen which sits atop the cooled wort when the yeast is pitched is quickly replaced with a layer of carbon dioxide once fermentation begins. Both of the methods mentioned above are easy and efficient. A two-stage fermentation system is recommended only when making a high-gravity beer like a barley wine or Doppelbock, which requires a fermentation period longer than two weeks, or when lagering (a period of prolonged maturation in the cold).

Because tap water contains oxygen, it should not be added to the fermenting or finished beer. Adding tap water increases the risk of oxidation and/or the introduction of bacteria.

The practices of taking daily hydrometer readings and skimming the hop resins off the fermenting wort are not recommended. Such practices allow oxygen and possible contamination to come in contact with the fermenting beer, which may produce undesirable results.

RACKING AND BOTTLING

Do not aerate or splash the beer when bottling. Siphon the beer off the sediment into a clean, sanitized container, taking care not to splash while siphoning. This will minimize the amount of oxygen that dissolves into solution and therefore reduce the acceleration of oxidation and the risk of contamination. Gently stir the priming syrup (three-quarters of a cup of corn sugar boiled with a small amount of water for 5 gallons of beer) into the beer, making sure it is thoroughly dispersed, but not agitated.

Gently siphon into clean, sanitized beer bottles and cap. Placing the siphon hose on the bottom of the beer bottle will reduce the volume of beer exposed to oxygen. Bottles should be filled to within one-half to one-and-a-half inches of the top. Purging the bottles with carbon dioxide prior to filling is an effective means of eliminating oxygen exposure, but it requires considerable effort. The greater the amount of oxygen left in the bottle, the faster the oxidation process will occur, which may result in prematurely stale-tasting beer.

OXYGEN BYPRODUCTS

The presence of oxygen at inappropriate points in the brewing process is ultimately to blame for beer staling, oxidation, excess diacetyl and ester levels, and aerobic contaminants.

The most important byproducts of fermentation are diacetyls (a buttery or butterscotch flavor in beer) and esters.

Ted Whippie (Left) and Brad Kraus (right), judging Best of Show.

Diacetyl can be formed by some bacteria, but it is always formed when there is oxygen in the wort. Therefore, diacetyl is a natural byproduct of yeast metabolism during the initial aerobic phase. After respiration, there should be no further diacetyl production unless oxygen is reintroduced. During fermentation while the yeast is still in suspension, diacetyls are reduced. Esters are the fruity aromas such as strawberry, banana and grapefruit in the finished beer. Poor oxygenation of the cooled wort will lead to increased ester production.

Acetic acid bacteria (acetobacter), film yeast (candida) and several other wild yeasts require oxygen for growth. These "bugs" usually grow on or near the surface of the beer where there is more oxygen. Leaving a large air space in fermenters and bottled beers helps provide these organisms with the oxygen they require for growth. Using a closed fermentation system, which retains carbon dioxide in the headspace, helps to avoid aerobic contamination problems.

Air content is the biggest factor leading to oxidation in the finished package. When certain compounds in the finished beer oxidize they produce flavor characteristics such as cardboardy, sherrylike-winey and pineappley. The reaction most commonly associated with oxidation is the "vinegar process" (i.e., ethanol that is left exposed to oxygen for a significant period of time oxidizes to acetaldehyde and then to acetic acid). All beers are subject to flavor instability after bottling. Time, temperature and the amount of oxygen introduced during fermentation and bottling all affect the final beer flavor.

Oxidation and oxidation-reduction reactions occur throughout the brewing process. The major oxidation reactions in beer are:
- Melanoidin-mediated oxidation of fusel alcohols
- Oxidation of iso-alpha acids
- Oxidation of fatty acids
- Oxidation of polyphenols
- Strecker reactions
- Aldol condensation

Refer to *Principles of Brewing Science* by George Fix (1989) for a complete discussion of oxidation reactions.

SUMMARY

A cooled wort saturated with dissolved oxygen will promote healthy, rapid yeast respiration and growth. A lack of oxygen can result in a slow, sluggish, incomplete fermentation. But once fermentation has begun, great care should be taken to minimize the contact between oxygen and the fermenting or finished beer. Siphoning carefully and protecting the fermentation with an airlock will minimize oxygen introduction. Oxygen cannot be excluded from the process, but unnecessary risks of contamination and oxygen introduction should be avoided.

Alberta Rager, a founding member of the Kansas City Bier Meisters, has been brewing for seven years. She is one of the managing partners of Bacchus & Barleycorn Ltd. in Merriam, Kansas, is a BJCP National Beer Judge, and has conducted BJCP exam study sessions for four years. The numerous ribbons displayed in the shop, won in competitions all over the country, are evidence of her brewing skills.

REFERENCES AND BIBLIOGRAPHY

Broderick, H. M., Ed. (1977). *The Practical Brewer*. Madison, Wis.: Impressions, Inc.

Fix, G. (1989). *Principles of Brewing Science*. Boulder, Colo.: Brewers Publications.

Hunt, Brian (1984). Spoilage organisms. *The New Brewer*, 1:2, 9-10.

Miller, D. (1988). *The Complete Handbook of Home Brewing*. Pownal, Vt.: Storey Communications, Inc.

Monk, P. (1989). Yeast nutrients in brewing. *zymurgy*, 12:4, 25-27.

Papazian, C. (1991). *The New Complete Joy of Home Brewing*. New York: Avon Books.

Siebel, R. (1984) Taste the ultimate test. *The New Brewer*, 1:1, 7-12.

12. Brewing Lambic Beers Traditionally and at Home

Mike Sharp
Convener of The Internet Lambic Mailing List
Martin Lodahl
President, Gold Country Brewers Association

• What is a lambic beer?
• How is it made commercially?
• How can these commercial techniques be adapted for brewing at home?

Martin will address the first two of these questions, and Mike the last.

THE WINE OF THE COUNTRY

Ever wonder what that straw-colored liquid was that those grain farmers in Bruegel paintings poured from pottery pitchers? Michael Jackson (1988) has suggested that it was

179

Mike Sharp   Martin Lodahl

probably a lambic, a member of that ancient and honorable family of beers made in a small area of the Senne Valley, in and around Brussels. By (Belgian) Royal decree, the grain bill in a lambic must be at least 30 percent unmalted wheat, initial gravity must be at least 1.020 (5 °Plato), and the beer must be spontaneously fermented (Guinard, 1990). Primary fermentation traditionally is conducted in wooden barrels (though some brewers ferment in bulk), and a single wort can be used to produce a broad range of finished beers, some refermented with fruit, some blended and refermented in a technique closely resembling the *methode champenoise*, and some aged in the cask. Lambics are by their nature crisp and tangy, with a pleasing lactic sourness accented by light acetic notes, and made interesting by elements that even seasoned sensory evaluation specialists find difficult to describe. The adjectives most often applied include horsy, old leather and mousy, though none of these does justice to the delightful complexity of a well-made lambic.

MEET THE FAMILY

The most common lambic variants are gueuze, kriek, framboise, cassis and pêche, though enterprising brewers have experimented with many others. Though Americans are more familiar with the fruit lambics, the crowning achievement of the lambic brewer's art is gueuze, a blend of young and aged lambics. At Cantillon, the most traditional of the handful of surviving lambic breweries, the beers used in gueuze are one, two and three years old. Each of these beers contributes its unique characteristics to the final blend. The vigorous carbonation for which gueuze is noted results from the refermentation of the youngest beer. The bottles used are similar to Champagne bottles with a raised punt for strength, and are both corked and crown-capped. Gueuze is traditionally aged from six months to a year, including at least one summer, to "marry" the flavors and to condition. Cantillon stretches that aging period to two years.

Fruit lambics are customarily young lambics refermented in the barrel with whole fruit, though in recent years (and for certain fruits) some breweries have made considerable use of juices, syrups and concentrates. The secondary fermentation was traditionally allowed to continue until completion, though now some less traditional brewers pasteurize before this fermentation is complete, producing a much sweeter and less complex beer. Some of these fruit lambics (especially, apparently, those intended for the American market) are so intensely sweet that the invigorating sourness lambics are known for is completely masked. The names indicate the fruit used: kriek is Flemish for cherry, framboise French for raspberry, cassis French for black currant, and pêche French for peach.

The last century has seen dramatic shifts in the fortunes of lambics. Before 1885, lambic was virtually the Belgian national drink, with *mars* (a low-gravity table beer once made from second runnings of a lambic mash) a regular staple of most households. In Brussels, there was a cafe for every five and three-quarters inhabited dwellings (Jef Lambic, undated), and virtually all of them served lambics! The "Brown Invasion" of Bavarian and British beers in the last years of the 19th century shook to its roots the elaborate network of brewers, blenders and merchants of these remarkable beers. The high production cost of lambics left them at a competitive disadvantage, especially after World War II when changing tastes and fashions relegated lambics to the role of a rustic throwback. Happily they have survived and are making something of a comeback, but they are still far from being mainstream products.

HOW LAMBICS ARE BREWED COMMERCIALLY

The reasons for the high cost (and quality) of lambics are perhaps clearest at the Cantillon Brewery in Brussels. Operated as a non-profit foundation (Musee Bruxellois de la Gueuze ASBL), this brewery has retained a completely traditional approach to lambic brewing. Tours, and the brewery's outstanding products, are offered between 10 a.m. and 5 p.m. on Saturdays from October through April at Rue Gheude 56, Brussels. At Cantillon it is clear that the process of producing a lambic is long and labor intensive, especially if traditional methods are used. The authors are convinced that these traditional methods produce the best results, an opinion shared by many of the most avid lambic enthusiasts.

The brewing process at Cantillon begins in a dry and airy loft, where sacks of pale, two-row malted barley are stored along with sacks of soft, light-colored unmalted wheat. The grain (wheat first, then malt) is weighed and poured down a chute to the mill on the floor below. The cracked grains (35 percent wheat, 65 percent malted barley) drop one more floor to the mash-tun, fashioned from copper and insulated with wood staves. The mash is agitated in the tun by elaborate rake-like arms. A combination of additions of boiling water and two decoctions (where a portion of the mash is pumped into an adjacent cooker, boiled and returned) is used to raise the temperature from 122 degrees F (50 degrees C) to 167 degrees F (75 degrees C) over a period of two and a half hours. The mash is then allowed to settle, and the wort is drained off through the slotted bottom of the mash-tun, while a sprinkler-like arrangement called a Scotch cross is fitted above the tun to gently distribute the sparge water. The collected wort is pumped into the boiling kettle. Because of the unmalted wheat, the wort will be turbid, and high in dextrins and starches, but the unique nature of a lambic fermentation makes that no disadvantage. The substantial additions of boiling water to the mash make the final wort extremely thin.

The boiling kettle is also made of copper, is insulated with what appears to be a mineral substance, and rises from its base just over the mash-tun up through the floor above, next to the grain mill. Huge steam coils provide the heat, and a large propeller-like dasher provides agitation. The cooker used in the decoction mash is a nearly identical unit located a few steps away. During the boil of three and a half hours or more, the hops are added.

Aged (*surannees*) hops are one of the unusual features of lambics. The emphasis of the flavor profile is on sourness rather than bitterness, so, though hops are used in relatively large quantities for their preservative value, they are first aged from two to three years to remove as much of their flavor as possible. Even though the lambic style predates the use of hops in beer, hops have long been considered indispensable in lambics, despite the somewhat brutal treatment they are given. The appropriately named Jef Lambic, in his amusing and informative autobiography, describes how a sudden jump in the price of hops in 1883 caused his brewer father to conclude that the end of the world (figuratively speaking, presumably) was near!

At the end of the boil, the bitter wort is drained into a copper hop back, and then is gently pumped up to a cooling tun in the attic, where the most distinctive part of the process takes place: "pitching" the wort by exposing it to wind-borne microflora. The cooling tun is a shallow copper pan set just under the roof, in a room whose "walls" consist of open slats. Here, clearly, is the reason this brewing style is limited to such a small region. The unique flavor of lambics is due to the "local rot"; a sharp, lambic-like tang is clearly identifiable in the odors of standing water in Brussels. So dependent is the fermentation process on the composition of ambient microflora that lambics are only brewed in the cooler months, when microbiological conditions are favorable. The wort is left to cool overnight, and by morning is near 72 degrees F (22 degrees C), and ready for racking. First it is drained from the cooling tun into a copper mixing tun, a step I suspect is to homogenize the wort after it has stratified during the long cooling rest, and to facilitate trub removal. The cooling tun is constructed with a sump and floating pickup to aid in separation.

From the mixing tun, the beer is moved by gravity to barrels in the cellar. These barrels, frequently old wine barrels, have had the bung recut into a rectangle nearly as wide as the stave. The inside of the barrels are cleaned and scraped with hot water, stick brushes known as *ramones*, and an amazing, mediaeval-looking device that swings sharpened chains.

When staves split or rot they are replaced with staves from junked barrels; much effort goes into maintaining the cooperage. Each barrel has its own microbiological contribution to make. Because the bungs are left open during primary fermentation, the environment within the brewery makes its contribution as well. Many brewers who learned Pasteur-inspired brewing methods find this practice disturbing, and are especially horrified by the sight of barrels festooned with spider webs. They shouldn't be. In conventional breweries, spiders are banished to control biological contaminants. They are encouraged in lambic breweries, because they reduce the population of fruit flies, known vectors of acetic acid bacteria. Some acetic acid content is appropriate in the lambic flavor profile, but it should not be too strong.

As primary fermentation begins (typically three days after cooling), the froth pours through the open bung and down the sides of the barrel, hardening to form an effective porous seal. During this time, the dominant fermentation agents are enteric bacteria and the wild yeast *Kloeckera apiculata*, both of which are soon displaced by yeast of the *Saccharomyces* genus, usually *S. bayanus* or *S. cerevisiae* (Guinard, 1990). After activity subsides, the barrels are cleaned up and topped off, and the bung closed with four plies of corduroy held in place by a small wooden billet. This is the time that the more fastidious organisms, including the bacteria *Pediococcus damnosus*, wild yeast of the *Brettanomyces* genus, and oxidative yeast of a variety of other genera begin to develop significant populations. This phase of fermentation frequently lasts a year or longer.

Occasionally, the fermentation process goes farther than the brewer wishes. In extreme cases the lambic becomes so acidic that it is used to clean tuns and utensils. Usually, however, it can be recovered to the point where it is at least salable by blending it with a younger lambic, then briefly aging with some sugar and a few grains of rice and wheat (Lambic, undated).

When I went to Belgium, I had hoped to gain some insight into how I might recreate the unique flavor of lambics at home, through observing the methods of commercial producers. I had already concluded that there was more to it than adding bottle cultures to a light wheat wort. I learned quite a bit that I found interesting, but much less that I could actually use. Immediately after returning home I "met" Mike Sharp over the computer brewing forum Homebrew Digest. Immediately after that, Jean-Xavier Guinard's amazing book *Lambic* was published. My reaction to the book was (and remains) a study in mixed emotions: profound gratitude over having such a remarkable resource in one slender volume, coupled with the feeling that I had never before been so thoroughly "scooped"! The book has been of immense value in the brewing and culturing experiments that Mike and I have carried out since.

MAKING LAMBICS AT HOME

I was first introduced to lambics and Flanders browns a few years ago at a bar called Holmes & Watson in Troy, New York. Since that time I have been looking for a way to reproduce the flavor of a lambic at home. Initially I started with the sketchy details found in a few of Michael Jackson's old articles and in Michael Matucheski's (1989) article on scratch-brewing lambics. I began experimenting with fermentations in oak, using old hops, and trying out different yeasts. However, I did not begin to have success in duplicating the style until I stumbled upon the names of some of the yeast and bacteria that are found in a lambic's fermentation.

It's All in the Fermentation

As Martin mentioned, a lambic is the product of a number of wild fermentations. It is this series of fermentations, more than anything else, that gives a lambic its unique character. Without a way to reproduce these fermentations you can use the best ingredients and procedures but a lambic will never result. In fact, the end product will be very much like an American wheat beer or perhaps a fruit-flavored light ale. It certainly will have little, if anything, in common with a true Belgian lambic. Unfortunately, beers of this nature recently have been marketed all over the United States as lambics, resulting in much confusion about just what a lambic is.

At a minimum, three different cultures are necessary to make a pseudo-lambic. (I prefer the term pseudo-lambic for my beers since a true lambic can only be made in Belgium.) These three cultures are *Saccharomyces cerevisiae*, *Pediococcus damnosus*, and *Brettanomyces bruxellensis* or *lambicus*.

Saccharomyces cerevisiae is the first organism that plays a major role in the fermentation. It is the primary fermenter of the wort, and it converts the bulk of the sugars. Its role in the fermentation of a lambic is similar to its role in other home-brew fermentations, but this yeast contributes little to the final character of the lambic. In fact, I have found that my choice of *S. cerevisiae* (English, European, alt, etc.) makes very little difference. In my batches, any character given to the beer by the *S. cerevisiae* always seems to be stripped off by the later fermentations. I've even gone so far as to test this with very distinctive yeasts, such as the one used to make Chimay, and I've always had similar results.

The second major fermentation of the wort is performed by *Pediococcus damnosus*, a lactic acid producing bacteria and a very slow-growing organism that has complex nutritional

Homebrewers peruse the exhibits at the beer and brewing exposition during club night.

requirements. It becomes prominent in the wort about three to four months into the fermentation and after the primary fermentation (Guinard, 1990). Frequently a disorder referred to as ropiness will form during this stage of the fermentation. Ropiness can be described as a thick convoluted layer of long strands floating on top of the fermenting beer. Although this is not aesthetically pleasing it is harmless. Further, it is likely to be broken down by the *Brettanomyces*.

P. damnosus is usually greatly feared as a brewery contaminant because it can spoil hopped wort and can be quite difficult to remove from a large-scale brewery (Fix, 1989; and Hough, Briggs & Young, 1982). However, experiments to date have shown that this bacteria is easily controlled in a home brewery through the use of a standard bleach solution. This is true for both Martin and me, as well as for a number of readers of the Internet lambic mailing list. I would recommend, however, avoiding plastic equipment because it can scratch easily and possibly provide a safe haven for the bacteria. This guideline applies not only fermenters, but to any equipment that comes into contact with the beer after fermentation (racking equipment, hoses, etc.). I believe that *P. damnosus* can be controlled in a home brewery because everything can be completely immersed in a bleach sanitizer (should it be necessary), while an equivalent procedure cannot be carried out in a large brewery. In short, there are many fewer places for the *Pediococcus* to hide in a home brewery.

Following the *P. damnosus* fermentation, *Brettanomyces* yeast takes over. The dominant yeast may be either *B. bruxellensis* or *B. lambicus* depending on the location of the brewery—*B. bruxellensis* is dominant in the city of Brussels and *B. lambicus* is dominant in the country. Both of these cultures lend distinct characteristics to lambics. Among these characteristics are horsiness and blanket-like aromas.

Brettanomyces is dominant in the fermenting lambic after about eight months (Guinard, 1990). During this stage of the fermentation any ropiness formed by *P. damnosus* will be broken down, and a thin waxy pellicle will be formed. As is the case with *P. damnosus,* this yeast is very slow-growing.

Care and Feeding of Exotic Cultures

In general the *Brettanomyces* cultures can be kept in the same way a *Saccharomyces* culture would be kept; that is, on a wort-based agar slant. The only change I make to this medium is to add 1 percent calcium carbonate ($CaCO_3$) to balance the production of acetic acid. I have kept cultures in this form for over six months under refrigeration.

P. damnosus is a bit more difficult to work with. It prefers to grow anaerobically (in the absence of oxygen), so I keep it in a liquid culture. It is difficult to plate out and check for contamination because the single colonies are very small when grown in the presence of oxygen. Further, regardless of the medium, it should be buffered against the buildup of lactic acid. I generally do this by adding 1 percent $CaCO_3$ to the medium. Finally, although it is not strictly necessary, I use a commercial medium referred to as Difco lactobacilli MRS broth, which is specially formulated to meet some of the complex nutritional requirements of *Pediococcus.* Martin has had some reasonable success adding 1 percent $CaCO_3$ and 10 percent tomato juice to a standard wort solution.

Making a starter culture for either *Pediococcus* or *Brettanomyces* is very similar to making one for a culture of *S. cerevisiae.* The one exception is knowing when the culture is ready for pitching. I have generally found that a starter of *P. damnosus* will take about four days to one week to prepare. When it is ready it will have a uniform cloudiness throughout with the exception of the top one-eighth inch of liquid, which will be perfectly clear. The starter will also have a very sharp nose that is unmistakable once you've smelled it. A *Brettanomyces* starter behaves in much the same way, but it will settle out much more quickly than the *Pediococcus.*

Sour Mashing: A Way to Make Lambics?

Sour mashing has occasionally been suggested as a safe way to obtain a lambic-like beer without the worry of using *Pediococcus.* Under ideal situations this may be true, but one of the contributors to the lambic mailing list, Aaron Birenboim, explored this possibility with little success. One of the major difficulties was obtaining the correct sourness. Since sour mashing is effectively a wild fermentation like those used in making a real lambic, its success depends on the proper microbiological climate. Unfortunately, it is not easy to control the souring organisms. The results of Aaron's test batches as well as the apparent controllability of *Pediococcus* on a home-brewing scale led us to abandon the sour mashing approach in favor of fermentation with *Pediococcus.*

It should be noted that we have not explored using a sour mashing approach with a *Pediococcus* culture; that is, performing a standard sour mash but innoculating the mash with a culture of *P. damnosus* and then covering the mash. This procedure could provide a way to control the acidity of the wort while insuring the proper souring organisms. It also would limit the possibility of exposing your fermenters and other brewing equipment to *Pediococcus.*

Other Souring Techniques

There is another method of souring wort, but it requires access to food-grade lactic and acetic acids. It is possible that

Pediococcus could be eliminated entirely and these acids added to the wort instead. This method was tried by Tom Gorman of the Wort Processors. The resulting beer, while sour, was only slightly so and lacked the complexity of a true lambic. However, in all fairness, Gorman did not use *Brettanomyces* in his batch, and this certainly contributed to the lack of complexity.

This method of making a pseudo-lambic raises the question of which acids are best to add. It is currently believed that a more diverse mixture of acids should be used for this approach, but I don't know of anyone who has experimented along these lines. Guinard's (1990) analysis of various lambics should be very useful to anyone wishing to explore this approach.

The Grain Bill

Traditionally a lambic is made of at least 30 percent unmalted wheat. Taking Cantillon as an example, a normal mixture might be 35 percent unmalted wheat and 65 percent two-row barley. Jef Lambic described a grain bill that had equal quantities of wheat and barley. Regardless of the quantity, the wheat generally contributes little to the overall sugars extracted from the mash. Rather, it provides a large amount of starch and protein, which are then broken down in later fermentations.

The wheat traditionally used is of the soft white summer variety. Not only is it used unmalted, but it also is not gelatinized prior to brewing. What little gelatinization occurs in the traditional brewing process would seem to be a result of the decoction. Neither Martin nor I have verified this, however, because we both use a step-mash technique.

Guinard has experimented with unmalted wheat, but

suggests that it be gelatinized before brewing. Martin has tried using wheat flakes, and I have experimented with malted wheat. Unfortunately there are too many variables between all of the batches to draw any conclusions as to the contributions (or lack thereof) of any of these methods.

Keep Those Old Hops!

As Martin mentioned, the hops used in a lambic are aged to lessen their bittering ability and aroma. This is done because the lambic brewer is interested mainly in the hop's preservative qualities. As for the variety of hops, Jackson (1991) makes note of seeing Belgian-grown Brewer's Gold, British Fuggles and Bohemian Saaz in lambic breweries. Guinard (1990) reports encountering Northern Brewer, Bramling Cross, Bullion and Goldings.

One shortcut to the aging process has been separately explored by at least two people. One is Martin, and the other is Quentin B. Smith (1990). The technique involves drying the hops in an oven for a set period of time. Martin's technique is as follows: the hops are spread evenly over a baking sheet and baked for one hour at 300 degrees F. The hops are then removed from the oven and allowed to stand in the open air for three days. One word of warning though: make sure everyone at home likes the smell of hops!

Fermenting in the Wood

While it is not necessary to ferment in oak to make a pseudo-lambic, I would like to pass along my experiences with and techniques for using oak fermenters. First and foremost, expect a new cask to yield very harsh oak-flavored brews for its first few uses. In fact, I would go so far as to make inexpensive extract beer for the first few batches since you'll probably want to dump them after the fermentation.

I picked up most of my initial knowledge of cleaning and maintaining casks from a book on cider-making (Proulx & Nichols, 1980). Why? Apparently present-day cider makers still look upon casks as part of their tradition, while brewers seem to forget the days of casks and prefer to work with plastic, glass or stainless.

I use an uncoated 15-gallon American oak wine barrel as a fermenter. It was purchased at a local homebrew shop at no insignificant cost. Unfortunately, when I bought it I had no idea of what I was looking for. As a result, I purchased a cask that had dried out considerably and that leaked terribly. Only after a few weeks of soaking the cask and liberally applying wax to the leaks could I stop the leaking. From this experience I would strongly suggest that anyone purchasing a cask find out just how long it has been sitting around the shop.

Once the cask is watertight (it really should be when you purchase it), there is the matter of cleaning it. Recently I have been cleaning my cask with about three to four ounces of soda ash to each gallon of water and using enough water to fill the cask. I let this mixture sit for an hour or so, and then I drain the contents of the cask. I then neutralize the soda ash by putting a few gallons of a mixture of water, sodium metabisulfite (Campden tablets, two per gallon) and citric acid (about one-quarter ounce per gallon) in the cask, and rolling it around. Finally, after a few minutes of this treatment I rinse the cask well.

Generally I try to avoid storing the cask unused. After all, that would mean chancing a break in the supply of lambic! When it is necessary to store the cask for a period of time I fill it with a solution of water and Campden tablets, mainly to keep the cask from drying out.

One final word of advice to those thinking of working with casks. Remember that a full 15-gallon cask is heavy. Unless you lug engine blocks around for a workout I'd strongly suggest the purchase of a good pump.

RECIPES

A Sample Extract Recipe
(Mike Sharp)

This beer is a bit of a fake. While it has a lot of the characteristics of a lambic, it is based on just a few cans of Munton and Fison extract and some additional hops. It contains no umalted wheat, and Chimay yeast is used to ferment the wort. This batch was originally made to test the possibility of using extracts in making lambics, and as a quick way to help break in my cask. The recipe (for 15 gallons) is as follows:

Ingredients:
  6   3 1/3 pound cans of Munton and Fison wheat extract
  9   ounces aged Perle hops
     Water to make approximately 16 gallons total volume
         prior to boil (bottled spring water, chemistry
         unknown)
750   ml Chimay yeast starter
  2   cups *Pediococcus damnosus* starter
     Brettanomyces bruxellensis
1/4   cup light DME for priming
 15   pounds frozen raspberries

Procedure:
Mix the extract, hops and water, and boil for one hour. Allow to cool/settle for one hour and then transfer off the trub

to an oak cask. Cool overnight, then pitch the Chimay yeast starter. One week later, pitch the *Pediococcus damnosus* starter; ten days after that, pitch the *Brettanomyces bruxellensis*.

When I made this beer, I split the batch. After four months, I bottled 2 1/2 gallons, priming with 1/4 cup light DME. The remainder was racked into a stainless-steel keg with 15 pounds of frozen raspberries. The beer was allowed to ferment on the raspberries for about three months before kegging. During this entire process the cask ullage was filled as necessary with a previous batch of pseudo-lambic.

Sample All-grain Recipe
(Martin Lodahl, after Guinard (1990))

Ingredients:
       7 pounds two-row pale malted barley
3 1/2 pounds brewers' flaked wheat
   1/2 pound crystal malt
       1 ounce leaf hops (equal parts Chinook, Willamette and
                 Northern Brewer, baked 1 hour at 300 degrees F
                 and left 3 days in the open air)
          Wyeast No. 1007 (German ale) yeast
          Pediococcus damnosus culture
          Brettanomyces bruxellensis culture
          teaspoon yeast nutrient
   3/4 cup dextrose (for priming)

Procedure:
Mash-in using 14 quarts of 130 degree F (54.5 degree C) water, with 1 teaspoon gypsum added, for 5 minutes. Raise to 140 degrees F (60 degrees C) for protein rest and hold for 20 minutes. Raise to 155 to 158 degrees F (68 to 70 degrees C) and hold for 60 minutes. Mash out for 10 minutes at 170 degrees F

(76.5 degrees C). Sparge with 5 gallons of water, beginning at 170 degrees F (76. 5 degrees C) and rising to 190 degrees F (87.5 degrees C). pH should be 5.7. Boil 2 hours, with hops added near the beginning of the boil.

The first surprise was that the iodine starch test came out negative after only 30 minutes of mashing. The mash itself looked different: I began to understand what was meant by a turbid mash. The sparge wasn't nearly as crystalline as I'm accustomed to seeing it, despite an excellent set to the filter bed, and the boil produced a hot break virtually outside the realm of credibility! Fermentation with the ale yeast took off like the proverbial shot. The *P. damnosis* was pitched one week after the start of the fermentation, and *B. bruxellensis* was pitched two weeks after that, when the ferment became ropy.

ACKNOWLEDGMENTS

The authors would like to thank those who both know-ingly and unknowingly contributed to this paper. First and foremost is Jean-Xavier Guinard. Without his initial work on lambics as well as our many phone conversations we never would have progressed this far. We would also like to thank Aaron Birenboim for sharing his results on sour-mashed "lambics," Tom Gorman for sharing his results on the use of food-grade lactic acid, Sheri Almeda for helping to answer some questions about the production of lactic acid by *Pediococcus* and for pointing us towards the proper literature, the members of the Wort Processors and the Gold Country Brewers Association for putting up with weird (and not al-ways drinkable) beer, and the members of the lambic mailing list for sanity-checking our crackpot ideas.

Michael D. Sharp *is a temporary resident of scenic, cultural downtown Lowell, Massachusetts, while awaiting a move to Beaverton, Oregon, where he will continue his work on a doctorate in computer science. He has been brewing for about three years and has been working on recreating the lambic style in the United States for two years. Being a student, in his spare time he has no spare time, and hence his only known hobbies are studying, brewing when completely burnt out, and studying. Mike hopes to change a lot of this in the near future.*

Martin A. Lodahl *is proud to be both a carbon-based life form and a member of Sacramento's Gold Country Brewers Association. He is a systems analyst for Pacific Bell in Oakland, and lives and brews in the old gold-mining town of Auburn. When not inflicting his weird brews on the unsuspecting, he is tending his hop garden with his wife Claudia, and children Natasha and Sebastian.*

REFERENCES

Guinard, J. (1990). *Lambic.* Boulder, Colo.: Brewers Publications.

Fix, G. (1989). *Principles of Brewing Science.* Boulder, Colo.: Brewers Publications.

Hough, J. S., Briggs, D. E., and Young, T. W. (1982). *Malting and Brewing Science, Vol. 2.* New York: Chapman and Hall.

Jackson, M. (1991). *The Great Beers of Belgium.* Antwerp, Belgium: Media Marketing Communications.

Jackson, M. (1988). *New World Guide to Beer.* Philadelphia: Running Press.

Lambic, J. (undated). *Les Memoires de Jef Lambic.* Brussels: Editions "La Technique Belge."

Matucheski, M. (1989). Scratch brewing the Belgian browns, *zymurgy,* 12:2, 25-29.

Proulx, A., and Nichols, L. (1980). *Sweet and Hard Cider.* Pownal, Vt.: Garden Way Publishing.

Smith, Q. B. (1990). Matching hops with beer styles, *zymurgy,* 13:4, 55-60.

APPENDIX
Resources

Suppliers of Cultures for Lambics

G.W. Kent (wholesale only—contact your local shop)
3691 Morgan Rd.
Ann Arbor, MI 48108
(313) 572-1300

University of California at Davis
Department of Food Science, Brewing Lab
Davis, CA 95616

The Internet Lambic Mailing List

For subscription requests: lambic-request@cs.ulowell.edu
For article submissions: lambic@cs.ulowell.edu

13. Setting Up Your Home Draft System

Dave Miller
Author, The Complete Handbook of Home Brewing

Recently, I became brewmaster at the St. Louis Brewery, the first brewpub in Missouri. When I got involved in the project one of the jobs I was given was to help with the design of our draft beer system. Fortunately, Gary Bauer of BRD Inc. designed and built our brewing equipment, and I was able to tap into his expertise. I want to give him full credit right now—everything you'll learn here from me, I learned from Gary.

When I learned how draft systems in bars and restaurants are designed, I realized why homebrewers have so much trouble with their draft systems. You know the kind of problems I'm talking about—carbonation that's too high (or too low), beer that shoots out of the tap at a hundred miles an hour or foams like a mad dog. I've seen all these problems among my homebrewing friends—and in my own draft system, too, I hasten to add.

Dave Miller

So let's do it—let's set up a draft system that delivers properly carbonated beer at the proper temperature and at a moderate flow rate, one that lets you put as much of a head of foam on the beer as you want when you pour it. It's likely that the only new equipment you'll need is some new beer hose. You've already spent hundreds on your draft system; all you need to make it perfect is a couple of hours and a pocket calculator.

Let's begin with carbonation, which most of you already understand. Some of you may still be using the "great big bottle" method—that is, you prime your draft kegs with sugar or wort and carbonate them like bottled homebrew. This method creates a number of problems. First of all, you get a fair amount of yeast in the bottom of the keg. That means beer loss; either you have to draw off a couple of quarts of cloudy beer when you tap the keg, or you have to cut off the draw tube so that you can leave the sediment in the keg. You also get cloudy beer every time you move the keg around. In addition, carbonation level is hard to control precisely. You usually end up having to adjust it by letting some gas blow off, then wait a couple of days for the beer to settle down.

Because of these problems, I much prefer artificial carbonation. Whether or not you filter your beer, if you chill it in the carboy before transfer, most cultured yeast strains will drop out nicely and allow you to rack almost yeast-free beer into your keg. Of course, if you use a powdery yeast like

Wyeast No. 1007, you will have to filter it to get a yeast-free beer.

I know there is a lot of folklore in the homebrewing community about the benefits of natural carbonation and leaving the yeast in contact with the beer. Some of it is true, especially regarding the antioxidant properties of yeast. In addition, strong ales seem to gain in complexity and smoothness if they stay in contact with yeast during storage. But for most styles of beer—including all lagers—yeasty flavors are not desirable, and the best way to avoid them is to separate the beer from the yeast as soon as the period of lagering or secondary fermentation is over.

My recommendation for draft beer is to let it ferment out, then transfer it to the carboy for a period of cold storage at about 34 degrees F (1 degree C). You only need about five days for ales—enough time to drop the yeast out. For lagers, two or three weeks is better. Then filter it if you wish. (There are a number of good articles describing filtering procedures; the subject is outside the scope of this talk.) Finally, carbonate the beer artificially following Byron Burch's method (as outlined in Burch, 1990, pp. 180-185).

OK. You have yeast-free, properly carbonated homebrew in your keg. What could go wrong? Plenty. Remember that when you carbonated your beer, you set the head pressure according to the beer temperature, then agitated the beer to dissolve CO_2 in it. When you do this, the CO_2 dissolves out of the headspace into the beer so that the internal pressure—that is, the pressure of the gas dissolved in the beer—balances the pressure of the gas in the headspace. At this point no more gas will dissolve, and the beer is carbonated to the number of volumes shown in the carbonation chart (Table 1).

But what happens when we change the temperature? The system can get out of balance. For example, suppose we

TABLE 1
Volumes of Carbon Dioxide (CO_2)

Pounds per square inch (psi)

Beer Temp (°F)	1	2	3	4	5	6	7	8	9	10	11	12	13	14	15	16	17	18	19	20	21	22	23	24	25	26	27	28	29	30
30	1.82	1.92	2.03	2.14	2.23	2.36	2.48	2.60	2.70	2.82	2.93	3.02																		
31	1.78	1.88	2.00	2.10	2.20	2.31	2.42	2.54	2.65	2.76	2.86	2.96																		
32	1.75	1.85	1.95	2.05	2.16	2.27	2.38	2.48	2.59	2.70	2.80	2.90	3.01																	
33		1.81	1.91	2.01	2.12	2.23	2.33	2.43	2.53	2.63	2.74	2.84	2.90	2.96																
34		1.78	1.86	1.97	2.07	2.18	2.28	2.38	2.48	2.58	2.68	2.79	2.89	3.00																
35			1.83	1.93	2.03	2.14	2.24	2.34	2.43	2.52	2.62	2.73	2.83	2.93	3.02															
36			1.79	1.88	1.99	2.09	2.20	2.29	2.39	2.47	2.57	2.67	2.77	2.86	2.96															
37				1.84	1.94	2.04	2.15	2.24	2.34	2.42	2.52	2.62	2.72	2.80	2.90	3.00														
38				1.80	1.90	2.00	2.10	2.20	2.29	2.38	2.47	2.57	2.67	2.75	2.85	2.94														
39					1.86	1.96	2.05	2.15	2.25	2.34	2.43	2.52	2.61	2.70	2.80	2.89	2.98													
40					1.82	1.92	2.01	2.10	2.20	2.30	2.39	2.47	2.56	2.65	2.75	2.84	2.93	2.99												
41						1.87	1.97	2.06	2.16	2.25	2.35	2.43	2.52	2.60	2.70	2.79	2.87	2.96	3.00											
42						1.83	1.93	2.02	2.12	2.21	2.30	2.39	2.47	2.56	2.65	2.74	2.82	2.91	3.00											
43							1.90	2.00	2.08	2.17	2.25	2.34	2.43	2.51	2.60	2.69	2.78	2.86	2.95											
44							1.86	1.95	2.04	2.13	2.21	2.30	2.38	2.47	2.55	2.64	2.73	2.81	2.90	2.99										
45							1.82	1.92	2.00	2.09	2.18	2.25	2.34	2.42	2.50	2.59	2.67	2.75	2.84	2.93	3.02									
46								1.88	1.96	2.05	2.14	2.22	2.30	2.38	2.46	2.54	2.62	2.70	2.78	2.86	2.94	3.03								
47								1.84	1.92	2.00	2.08	2.15	2.23	2.30	2.38	2.45	2.53	2.61	2.69	2.77	2.85	2.93	3.01							
48								1.80	1.88	1.96	2.05	2.13	2.21	2.29	2.36	2.44	2.52	2.60	2.67	2.75	2.83	2.91	2.98							
49									1.85	1.93	2.01	2.10	2.18	2.25	2.34	2.42	2.50	2.58	2.66	2.74	2.83	2.91	2.99							
50									1.82	1.90	1.98	2.06	2.14	2.21	2.30	2.38	2.45	2.54	2.62	2.70	2.78	2.86	2.94	3.02						
51										1.88	1.96	2.03	2.11	2.18	2.26	2.33	2.41	2.49	2.57	2.64	2.72	2.80	2.88	2.97						
52										1.84	1.91	1.99	2.06	2.14	2.22	2.30	2.37	2.45	2.54	2.61	2.69	2.76	2.84	2.93	3.00					
53										1.80	1.88	1.96	2.03	2.10	2.18	2.26	2.33	2.41	2.48	2.57	2.64	2.72	2.80	2.88	2.95	3.03				
54											1.85	1.93	2.00	2.07	2.15	2.22	2.29	2.37	2.44	2.52	2.60	2.67	2.75	2.83	2.90	2.98				
55											1.82	1.89	1.97	2.04	2.11	2.19	2.25	2.33	2.40	2.47	2.55	2.63	2.70	2.78	2.85	2.93	3.01			
56											1.86	1.93	2.00	2.07	2.15	2.21	2.29	2.36	2.43	2.50	2.58	2.65	2.73	2.80	2.88	2.96	2.99			
57												1.83	1.90	1.97	2.04	2.11	2.18	2.25	2.33	2.40	2.47	2.54	2.61	2.69	2.76	2.84	2.91	2.99	3.01	
58												1.80	1.86	1.94	2.00	2.07	2.14	2.21	2.29	2.36	2.43	2.50	2.57	2.65	2.72	2.80	2.86	2.94	3.01	
59													1.83	1.90	1.97	2.04	2.11	2.18	2.25	2.32	2.39	2.46	2.53	2.60	2.67	2.75	2.81	2.89	2.96	3.03
60													1.80	1.87	1.94	2.01	2.08	2.14	2.21	2.28	2.35	2.42	2.49	2.56	2.63	2.70	2.77	2.84	2.91	2.98

Draw a line straight across from the temperature of the beer to the desired volumes of CO_2 then straight up to find the correct psi of your regulator.

carbonated a lager beer at 34 degrees F (1 degree C) to 2.5 volumes. That means 9 psi in the headspace. But suppose we want to serve the beer at 42 degrees F (5.5 degrees C). Figuring that the beer's temperature will rise 2 degrees when it is poured into the glass, we should dispense it at 40 degrees F (4.5 degrees C). So we put it in a refrigerator set to that temperature. Now, as the beer temperature rises, it won't hold as much gas. What we find from Table 1 is that we will need 12 psi of head pressure in order to maintain our 2.5 volumes of carbonation. If we only apply 9 psi, gas will come out of solution until the pressures equalize, and eventually the carbonation level will drop to 2.2 volumes—a little low for lager. Also, if we try to dispense the beer at 9 psi, the beer will be losing gas as it flows through the line, and that means foaming.

So far, smooth sailing. Most homebrewers know that they have to set their head pressure according to the temperature of the beer in the keg. But what happens when we try to dispense the beer under 12 psi? With most home draft systems, we get a flow rate more suitable to a fire extinguisher than to beer delivery. The beer gushes out so hard that its collision with the bottom of the glass causes tremendous agitation and splashing. As a result, most of the gas breaks out of solution and you end up with a glassful of foam.

In other words, low head pressure and high flow rate both lead to the same result—a glassful of foam instead of beer. And it gets worse. It is perfectly possible that a head pressure low enough to cause foaming will also be high enough to cause high flow rate. It takes at most 2 to 3 psi to move beer through a bar tap at a rate of one gallon per minute, which most bartenders and other experts consider ideal. And it takes virtually no pressure to move it through a "cobra head" soda tap at that rate.

How to get around this dilemma? Before we can do that, we have to understand why we are facing it. The key to the problem is the fact I just mentioned: that it only takes a little bit of pressure to push beer through a tap at a reasonable rate. Yet we all know that most pubs dispense their beer under 12 to 15 psi. How do they get away with it? Why doesn't the pressure propel the beer out at the speed of sound?

The answer is restriction. Pub draft systems are designed so that the restriction in the beer line gives a gentle flow of beer. There are two things that restrict beer flow through a line. The first is lift. It takes one psi of pressure to lift beer two feet vertically. So unless your beer line is perfectly horizontal from keg to tap, the first thing you have to figure out is the restriction imposed by lift.

The other source of restriction is simply the line itself. This depends upon both the material the line is made from and the line's inside diameter. Table 2 shows restriction per foot of line for common sizes and materials. You will notice that the material makes relatively less difference with the bigger diameter lines. If you are wondering what your draft line is made from, polyethylene is the semi-opaque, relatively stiff type of plastic beverage hose. Vinyl is usually clear, though it may be of different colors. In any case, it is quite flexible.

How do we use this information about restriction to make our draft system work correctly? The key is balance. We have to design our system so that the restriction of our run exactly equals the head pressure in our keg. Say we want to dispense lager at 40 degrees F (4.5 degrees C), carbonated to 2.5 volumes. First we set up our run so that the total restriction equals 12 psi. Then we hook up our gas line, and set the regulator to 14 psi (2 psi extra for the bar tap, remember). The beer should flow out the tap at one gallon per minute.

TABLE 2
Restriction (in pounds) for Different Line Widths (in inches)

Line length (feet)	Vinyl					Polyethylene		
	3/16	1/4	5/16	3/8	1/2	3/16	1/4	3/8
1	3	.85	.40	.20	.025	2.2	.50	.07
2	6	1.70	.80	.40	.050	4.4	1.00	.14
3	9	2.55	1.20	.60	.075	6.6	1.50	.21
4	12	3.40	1.60	.80	.100	8.8	2.00	.28
5	15	4.25	2.00	1.00	.125	11.0	2.50	.35
6	18	5.10	2.40	1.20	.150	13.2	3.00	.42
7	21	5.95	2.80	1.40	.175	15.4	3.50	.49
8	24	6.80	3.20	1.60	.200	17.6	4.00	.56
9	27	7.65	3.60	1.80	.225	19.8	4.50	.63
10	30	8.50	4.00	2.00	.250	22.0	5.00	.70
11	33	9.35	4.40	2.20	.275	24.2	5.50	.77
12	36	10.25	4.80	2.40	.300	26.4	6.00	.84
13	39	11.05	5.20	2.60	.325	28.6	6.50	.91
14	42	11.90	5.60	2.80	.350	30.8	7.00	.98
15	45	12.75	6.00	3.00	.375	33.0	7.50	1.05
16	48	13.60	6.40	3.20	.400	35.2	8.00	1.12
17	51	14.45	6.80	3.40	.425	37.4	8.50	1.19
18	54	15.30	7.20	3.60	.450	39.6	9.00	1.26
19	57	16.15	7.60	3.80	.475	41.8	9.50	1.33
20	60	17.00	8.00	4.00	.500	44.0	10.00	1.40
21	63	17.85	8.40	4.20	.525	46.2	10.50	1.47
22	66	18.70	8.80	4.40	.550	48.4	11.00	1.54
23	69	19.55	9.20	4.60	.575	50.6	11.50	1.61
24	72	20.40	9.60	4.80	.600	52.8	12.00	1.68
25	75	21.25	10.00	5.00	.625	55.0	12.50	1.75
30	90	25.50	12.00	6.00	.750	66.0	15.00	2.10
50	150	42.50	20.00	10.00	1.250	110.0	25.00	3.50
100	300	85.00	40.00	20.00	2.500	220.0	50.00	7.00
125	375	106.25	50.00	25.00	3.125	275.0	62.50	8.75
150	450	127.50	60.00	30.00	3.750	330.0	75.00	10.50

Table courtesy of The Cornelius Company

The system is perfectly balanced. We can pour out beer at a nice, reasonable rate, and we can put as much head on the beer as we want. Figure 1 shows an example of all the calculations needed.

FIGURE 1
Calculating Balance (Example)

STEP 1
Desired beer temperature = 40 degrees F (4.5 degrees C)
Desired carbonation level = 2.5 volumes
Pressure (from Table 1) = 12 psi

STEP 2
Lift (from middle of keg to tap) = 3 feet
Restriction = .5 L
     = .5 x 3
     = 1.5 psi

STEP 3
Length of run from keg to tap = 3.5 feet

STEP 4
Line restriction = Head pressure - Lift restriction
      = 12 - 1.5
      = 10.5 psi
If using a cobra head tap, add 2 psi (total = 12.5 psi in this case)

STEP 5
Correct material (from Table 2) is 3/16-inch vinyl tubing at 3 psi per foot.
10.5 psi / 3 = 3.5 feet required
12.5 psi / 3 = 4.17 feet (4 feet, 2 inches)

The system should be assembled using 3.5 feet (for a bar tap) or 4.17 feet (for a cobra head tap) of 3/16-inch vinyl tubing between the keg and the tap. If the regulator gauge is accurate, 14 psi should push the beer out at one gallon per minute.

Of course, in the real world there are likely to be some complications. The first one is that the cheap gauges found on most regulators are likely to be inaccurate. The gauges on our regulators at the St. Louis Brewery vary widely, some reading high and others low.

The easiest way to check your regulator gauge is to set up your draft system, following the steps I have described. Then fill a keg halfway with water or flat beer (better), close it, and hook it up to your regulator. Set the pressure correctly, then open the tap for exactly six seconds over a measuring pitcher. You should get 12 ounces of beer. If you get more, your regulator is reading low. If you get less, your regulator is reading high. Adjust the pressure and try again. But don't try to cut it too fine. You can drive yourself nuts trying to get it perfect.

The other complication is that beer taps vary. The little plastic cobra heads used by many homebrewers don't have nearly as much restriction as a regular bar tap. If you have a bar tap, a rule of thumb is that you will need to turn up the regulator 2 psi above the balance point to push the beer out the tap at one gallon per minute. With a cobra head, no additional pressure is needed, which means that you will have to add 2 psi of restriction to your line when you calculate your length.

By the way, I hope you know the correct method for setting a regulator. When you make any change—whether you are adjusting the pressure up or down—always begin by turning the screw counterclockwise until the pressure drops to zero. Then turn it clockwise until the pressure reading is correct. If you follow this method, you will be better able to repeat your results and you'll have less trouble with drift.

So there you have it. To balance a draft system, follow these steps:

1. Figure the head pressure in your keg.

2. Figure the total lift in your beer line. Measure from the middle of the keg to the bottom of your tap. Use the formula:

$$R \text{ (restriction in psi)} = 0.5 \text{ L (lift in feet)}.$$

3. Subtract lift from head pressure. If using a cobra head, add 2 psi to the figure. The result is the restriction that your line should impose.

4. Measure the horizontal length of your beer line from keg to tap. If the length is not critical—for example, if the tap is mounted on the top or side of your refrigerator—you can skip this step.

5. Select a line diameter and material that will give the correct restriction for the length of the run.

6. Finally, install the system, and set your regulator to deliver keg pressure plus 2 psi. Check to see that your flow rate is approximately one gallon per minute. This is equivalent to filling a 12-ounce glass in six seconds, or a 42-ounce pitcher in 20 seconds. Note this setting also.

You may be thinking that there is another variable we have to account for if this balancing act is really going to work, and you're right. I haven't accounted for temperature. In the real world, that beer line is liable to run through unrefrigerated space, which means that the temperature in the line will rise and, with it, the gas pressure in the beer itself. The gas will break out of solution and foam will come out the tap.

To avoid this problem, pubs run their beer lines inside a "python" of black foam tubing, and they employ some form of forced cooling to maintain the temperature inside the python. The two popular methods are air cooling and glycol cooling. Air cooling is simpler. Usually all that is involved is

Brewers check out the displays at the Saturday outdoor festival.

setting up a blower to force cold air out of the refrigerator or walk-in cooler and into the python. A second hose carries the cold air back to the cooler. Air cooling works well if the beer line run is short and direct.

For long or snaking runs, glycol cooling is preferable. This arrangement requires a small refrigeration unit that chills a glycol-and-water solution to the desired temperature—usually the temperature of the beer in the keg, or perhaps a degree or two colder. A pump circulates the glycol solution through a pair of lines inside the python.

I think you can understand that both of these methods, while perfectly feasible for homebrewers, can get pretty complicated and/or expensive. That is why I recommend a simpler system in which your beer tap(s) and beer line remain inside the refrigerator. If you follow this plan, you can use a convenient length of small diameter, restrictive beer line to impose most or all of the restriction you need.

If you want to get fancier, you can mount a beer tap on the side of a full size refrigerator. Probably the snazziest arrangement is to use a counter height refrigerator and mount a genuine brass bar column and tap on the top. With a little ingenuity, you could even add a drip tray to catch the spills. When mounting a bar tap, be sure to drill your hole big enough to allow cold air to circulate inside the column.

One difficulty with keeping the draft system inside a refrigerator is that it can only be balanced for one temperature and carbonation level. If you like to have more than one beer on tap at a time, you may need to use two regulators—one for ales and one for lagers. If you find yourself in this predicament, one way to save a little money is to buy secondary regulators rather than gas cylinders. These secondary regulators can be set to different working pressures as required by your different beers; your existing regulator becomes a primary regulator that should be set to about 45 psi. You balance each system independently. However, you still will be stuck with serving your ale and lager at the same temperature.

I have covered the main aspects of designing and setting up a draft system. However, there are some practical problems with day-to-day operation that I should mention. One is CO_2 pickup. Carbon dioxide dissolves readily in beer. You can carbonate a cold keg of beer in 15 minutes or so just by agitating it vigorously while applying head pressure. In most ways, that's good, and very convenient if you're in a hurry to tap a new batch.

But think for a minute about your carefully balanced draft system. Remember that when you are operating it, it is balanced only when the tap is open. The rest of the time, you are applying surplus head pressure—the working pressure that moves the beer out through the tap. Over time, this imbalance will seek to correct itself. Additional CO_2 will dissolve into the beer until the carbonation level (internal pressure) is equal to the head pressure.

A little extra carbonation may not make much difference to you. But to avoid gas break-out and foaming when you pour a beer, you will have to keep gradually increasing the head pressure to compensate for the dissolution of CO_2. This situation can get difficult if you take a few weeks to empty a keg.

There are a few ways to control the problem of CO_2 pickup. The first is to go through your kegs in a hurry. If you drink up a keg of beer in three or four days, the beer will not have time to pick up a significant amount of CO_2.

A second way is to use a mixture of carbon dioxide and nitrogen rather than straight carbon dioxide. At low pressures, nitrogen is practically insoluble in beer. Say we've got a keg of lager beer at 40 degrees F (4.5 degrees C) carbonated to 2.5 volumes. We already know that we need 12 psi of head pressure to maintain carbonation, and we have balanced our system so that the beer line imposes that much restriction. But we need to apply 14 psi, so that the beer will flow out the tap at the proper rate. What we can do is apply those additional 2 psi with nitrogen, by specifying a gas mix that is one-seventh nitrogen and six-sevenths carbon dioxide. That means that our 14 psi of head pressure will consist of 12 psi of carbon dioxide (which will maintain the carbonation level) plus 2 psi of nitrogen (which will push the beer out the tap).

You might think, intuitively, that as long as the total head pressure is 14 psi, the CO_2 would dissolve into the beer. But that doesn't happen. When you have a mixture of gases, each one behaves as if the others weren't there. Whether the total head pressure is 14 psi or 40 psi, if 12 of that is accounted for by CO_2, the CO_2 will behave as if the beer were under 12 psi.

You can set up a mixed gas system if you so desire. However, I feel that most homebrewers don't need this complication in their lives. Also, very few gas companies will agree to custom mix the small amounts of gas that you will require. The easiest way around the gas pickup problem is to simply adjust your regulator on an as-needed basis. In other words, keep the head pressure on your beer at the balance level. When you want to draw a few beers, turn it up so the beer will flow at the proper rate. When you have finished drawing your beer and you know you won't be having any more until the following evening, turn the pressure back down. This method is impractical for pubs but is perfectly workable in a home situation.

Dave Miller won the title Homebrewer of the Year in 1981. Since that time, he has written numerous articles and published several books, including The Complete Handbook of Home Brewing *(Storey, 1988) and* Continental Pilsener *(Brewers Publications, 1990). Dave is a Certified Beer Judge and a graduate of the Siebel Institute. He currently works as Brewmaster at The St. Louis Brewery, Inc. His fourth book,* Brewing the World's Great Beers, *was recently published by Storey Communications.*

REFERENCES

Burch, B. (1990). A great system for draft beers. In *Beer and Brewing, Vol. 10* (pp. 177-189). Boulder, Colo.: Brewers Publications.

14. Bock Talk

Ray Daniels
1991 Midwest Brewer of the Year (title co-holder)

We're here to talk about how to homebrew a great bock beer. Over the years that I have been homebrewing, I've had a lot of conversations about bock beer with brewers from the Chicago Beer Society and from other parts of the United States. But each of those discussions focused on a small part of the overall brew. I'm going to show you a series of analyses I have done on the best bock recipes that I could find. My goal in performing these analyses was to capture a complete understanding of all components of the brewing of these beers, from malt and hops to yeast and lagering. The analyses will help us understand how the best homebrewers go about creating great—and often award-winning—bock beers. When we're done, the objective is to take what we have learned and make a great bock beer of our own.

Ray Daniels

BOCK DEFINED

Before we get into the details of how to brew bock beer, we should first review the specifics of the style. Michael Jackson (1988) provides both good descriptions and some intriguing history of the style. We don't have room here to cover much of the history, so let's begin with his description. Jackson describes bock as a "strong lager served as a warming beer in late winter, early spring, or autumn, depending upon the part of the world," and says that it is "classically served at not less than 9 degrees C (48 degrees F) from a stoneware mug" (p. 12).

By the requirements of the German Reinheitsgebot, bocks must be strong beers with an original gravity of at least 1.066 (16.5 °Balling). Usually they are dark colored, but not as dark as a robust porter or a stout. The palate is strongly balanced toward malt and can exhibit a pronounced caramel flavor as well as some chocolate malt character. Although there is some black malt in the recipes we will review, it usually is added only in very small quantities for color. Most authorities agree that the style should not exhibit a noticeable black patent or roasted barley character. Bock beers also are characterized by a definite lager smoothness that can be achieved only through long periods of cold storage following fermentation. Fruitiness and esters are clearly inappropriate in this style.

In addition to bock itself, the bock style category includes Doppelbock, Helles or Maibock, and finally the super bock known as Eisbock. Some authors also recognize an American bock style. Doppelbocks are essentially just higher gravity versions of the basic bock. The Reinheitsgebot requires them to have a starting gravity of at least 1.074 (18.5 °Balling). The Helles and Maibock styles share the strength of the family, but come in lighter colors ranging from golden to nearly amber. They generally lack caramel and chocolate flavor tones and often display significant hop flavor. Eisbock is a super-test version of doppelbock produced by freezing the beer to remove water and increase the alcohol content.

I am going to limit this discussion to the main styles of bock and doppelbock because the recipes and brewing approaches are very similar.

COLLECTING THE RECIPES

To start this project, I collected all the bock homebrew recipes I could find. The first place I looked was in the *Winner's Circle*, a book of award-winning recipes published by the AHA (1989). Then I collected recipes from past issues of *zymurgy*. The recipes from these two sources should be of particular interest to us because the beers have been judged by a jury of our peers to represent the best bock beers entered into a national contest.

Knowing that many authors of homebrewing texts have already researched bock recipes for their own books, I also looked at what they had to offer. I consulted Charlie Papazian's (1984) *The Complete Joy of Home Brewing*, Dave Miller's (1988) *The Complete Handbook of Home Brewing*, Greg Noonan's (1986) *Brewing Lager Beer*, and Byron Burch's (1986) *Brewing Quality Beers*.

When I finished collecting the recipes, I had 23 different examples of ways that you could brew either a bock or doppelbock using a homebrew setup. Only one recipe was for an extract-only bock. Thirteen used some type of mixed grain/extract approach, and nine of the recipes were all-grain efforts. The recipes' sources are given in the Appendix.

EXALTED IN MALT

Bocks are a malt-dominant style, so the subject of malt is not quite as straightforward as it might be with some other styles. Bockmeisters can't even decide on what to use as base malt when taking the all-grain approach. The complexity of bock malt should not deter those who brew with extracts, however, because many award-winning bocks have been made using extract-based recipes. Let's start our discussion of how to brew this style by looking at the extract-only and extract-plus-specialty-grain recipes. Throughout this section, you may find it helpful to refer to Figures 1 and 2 (pp. 220-221), which show wort composition for the extract and all-grain recipes that were analyzed.

Extracts in Bock

As I mentioned, I found only one extract-only recipe. It used fairly unremarkable ingredients: 6 pounds (2.7 kilograms) of Munton and Fison light dry malt extract and 3.3 pounds (1.5 kilograms or one can) of John Bull amber unhopped malt extract syrup. This recipe gave the brewer an original gravity close to 1.065. Although the judges' comments on this beer noted that it was a bit thin and a little light on the malt, the recipe produced a good beer that took first place in the 1988 AHA competition.

The extracts used by those who brewed bocks with extract-based recipes include Alexander's, Munton and Fison and Bavarian Gold. Overall, it looks like the various types of Munton and Fison extract work well for extract-based bocks.

The specialty grains added to the extract-based brews included most of the same ones that we will see in the mash-based recipes: crystal, chocolate, black patent and toasted malt. These grain additions can be made either by adding them to the cold water and removing them right before the boil, or by steeping them at about 150 degrees F (65.5 degrees C) for 30 to 45 minutes.

Several of the recipes that I collected used extract in addition to a regular mash with malted barley. Most of these recipes were for doppelbocks, and the extract was used to boost the gravity into the appropriate range. If you make all-grain beers, you don't have to achieve all of your bock gravity with the grain—use some extract to put you over the hump. (Two of the four mash/extract recipes were AHA winners.)

Base Malt for All-grain Brews

The base malt is the grain that will make up 50 to 80 percent of the total grain bill for your beer. An examination of all-grain bock recipes fairly quickly yields two schools of thought on what should be the base malt for this brew. One group of authorities recommends two-row lager malt for this purpose, and another recommends Munich malt. Many recipes chose a point between the extremes, combining Munich and lager malt in various ratios. Figure 3 shows the Munich/lager mix used in the all-grain batches that I reviewed.

I've heard people say that you can't mash with Munich malt because it has no enzymes, but this is not true—I've done it! Dave Miller (1988) describes Vienna and Munich malt in his chapter on Pale Malts precisely because they both retain diastatic power after kilning and can be used as the basis for a

FIGURE 1
Wort Composition (% of total malt), Extract Brews

RECIPE NO.	10*	11*	13	12*	14	15	22	18	23	17	16	20*	19	21*
STYLE	Bock	Bock	Bock	Dop	Am	Am	Am	Var	Bock	Dop	Bock	Dop	Am	Dop
Extract:														
Light	65	67	94	63		83	30	62	59	31	57		47	53
Amber	35			27			52							
Dark		28			83							61		
Total	100	95	94	90	83	83	81	62	59	31	57	61	47	53
Malted barley											29	20	31	12
Malt + extract											86	80	78	65
Munich		2				4	23	18	54		4		18	
Crystal		2		4	10	4	4	15	14	15ᶜ	14ᵈ	2	4	6
Chocolate		2	6	2	3	4	7		3			2	3	6
Cara-pils							4		5			4		3
Black patent		1			3				1			2		
Other				4ᵃ		8ᵇ						4ᵉ	16ᶠ	3ᵍ
Gravity	1.064	1.065	1.063	1.078	1.045	1.039	1.055	1.080	1.065	1.080	1.066	1.074	1.043	1.085

10* 1988 AHA 1st place
11* 1987 AHA 2nd place
12* 1988 AHA 2nd place
20* 1984 AHA 1st place
21* 1987 AHA 1st place

a toasted
b toasted
c dark crystal
d dark crystal
e toasted
f flaked maize
g rolled wheat

FIGURE 2
Wort Composition (% of total malt), All-Grain Brews

RECIPE NO.	8	1*	4	3	6*	2*	5	9	7*
STYLE	Bock	Bock	Dop	Mai	Bock	Bock	Bock	Am	Bock
Malted barley	0	16	59	65	68	69	74	78	84
Munich	86	64	27	22	20	5	2	0	0
Crystal	14[a]	4	8	4	5	5	20[d]	4	12
Chocolate					3	2		3	
Cara-pils					3	5	5		
Black patent			8	9	1	1			4
Other		16[b]				14[c]		16[e]	
Gravity	1.066	1.074	1.076	1.067	1.049	1.078		1.043	1.063

1* 1990 AHA 1st place
2* 1989 AHA 1st place
6* 1985 AHA 1st place
7* 1986 AHA 1st place

[a] 90°L - 120°L crystal
[b] Vienna
[c] 1 pound toasted, 2 pounds wheat
[d] 20 ounces 90°L crystal
[e] flaked maize, dark crystal

FIGURE 3
Base Grain Selection

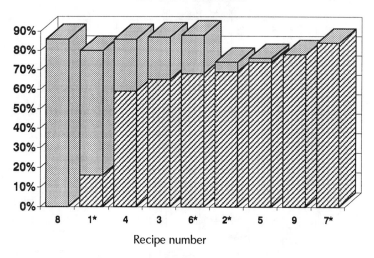

▦ Munich malt   ▨ Malted barley

recipe. The enzymes in Munich and Vienna malt are still hearty enough to handle conversion of their own starches; what they cannot do is convert adjuncts or non-enzymatic malts. This probably explains why most of the recipes use at least some lager malt along with Munich.

Maltsters produce Munich malt through a final kilning at a higher temperature (210 to 240 degrees F [99 to 115.5 degrees C]) than lager malt, which finishes between 130 and 180 degrees F (54.5 and 82 degrees C). As a result, Munich malt produces a deeper color, a fuller aroma and a rich caramel malt flavor in the finished beer. Darryl Richman made the first place bock in the 1990 AHA competition using Munich as the base malt. From my own experience with Munich- and lager-based bocks, I would have to say that I prefer the mostly-Munich approach.

When we look at Figure 3, we can divide the recipes into three groups. At the left are two recipes in which Munich malt makes up more than 60 percent of the grain bill. In the middle, there are three recipes that use 20 to 30 percent Munich malt. Finally, on the right, there are four recipes that use less than 5 percent of the grain. The stars next to the recipe numbers denote the AHA national homebrew competition winners. As you can see, they are fairly well divided among the three approaches.

Please note a couple of points about Munich malt. If you are going to use it as your base malt, be sure to use the best quality malt you can find. Many of the domestically produced Munich malts are made from six-row malt and have been reported to produce astringency when used in quantity. I recommend avoiding them for high quantity uses such as this. In addition, some brewers I have talked with have experienced "stuck mash" problems with Munich malt. If you encounter this difficulty, try giving the mash a 30 minute rest at about 95 degrees F (35 degrees C).

Specialty Malts: The Spice of Bock

You will find many combinations of specialty malts in widely varying quantities when looking at bock beer recipes. Picking the specialty malts you want and deciding how much of each to use is the fun part of making a bock. Winning brewers tended to use a little bit of every type of malt to provide complexity and character to their beers. This strategy has proved successful for other styles of beer as well, so keep it in mind as you put your own favorite recipe together.

The specialty malts found in bock recipes include crystal, chocolate, black patent, toasted, and wheat malts. I will discuss them in order of the frequency that they appear in the winning recipes.

Crystal Malt

Crystal was included in 20 of 23—or almost 90 percent—of the recipes that I examined. Please note that very dark crystal malt is recommended for bocks. It helps to provide the correct color as well as a deep caramel flavor to your bock. Without much trouble you should be able to find 90°L or 120°L crystal malt.

The big question with crystal is how much to use. In the recipes that I surveyed, crystal ranged from 2 to 20 percent of the grain bill (see Figure 4). The most frequently occurring usage was about 5 percent of the total grain—a formula that occurred in 10 of the 23 recipes. Another group of five recipes used about 15 percent crystal malt. Then there was a small cluster of points at 8, 10, and 12 percent crystal and, finally, the two outliers at 2 and 20 percent.

I suggest choosing between using 5 percent or 15 percent crystal. The higher quantities of crystal tended to be associated with lower quantities of Munich malt, so if you decide to

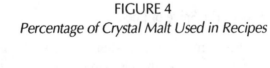

FIGURE 4

Percentage of Crystal Malt Used in Recipes

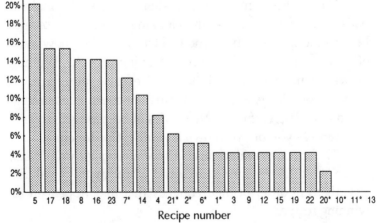

Recipe number

use two-row malt as your base grain, I would advise that you lean toward the higher amount of crystal malt. If you're starting out with 80 percent Munich, cut back the crystal to 5 percent of the grain bill.

Chocolate Malt

In my humble opinion, chocolate malt is a required component of any bock recipe. I like chocolate malt and I think that it imparts a flavor component that is characteristic of the style. But some people have other views. Only 75 percent of the recipes that I examined called for chocolate malt. Those who did not use chocolate malt in their formulations generally used higher quantities of crystal or of crystal *and* Munich to make up for the ommission.

On the question of quantity there wasn't much variation. All the recipes that specified chocolate malt called for it to compose 2 to 5 percent of the mash, which generally works out to 8 ounces (227 grams) or less for a 5-gallon (19-liter) batch.

Black Patent Malt

Now we enter the realm of optional grains for a successful bock formulation. Only seven of 23 recipes specified the use of black patent—that's about 30 percent. However, five of the seven who used it were AHA winners. Clearly judges who appraise bocks in these competitions have a taste for a little black patent.

When it was used, black patent composed only 1 or 2 percent of the total mash and it was almost always used in conjunction with chocolate and crystal malts. It is clear that black patent never plays a major role in the flavor profile of the beer. Instead, it contributes color and some complexity to the overall malt character.

Toasted Malt

Because malt dominates bock beers, richness and complexity in the character of the malt is important. I have already mentioned the fact that the winners tend to use a little bit of everything to achieve this complexity. Toasted malts are another way to add malt character and complexity to your beer. In my survey, I found four recipes using toasted malts, and three of these were AHA winners.

We can only guess about the specific toasting procedures followed by these brewers, but how they did it is probably far less important that the fact that they did. You can follow any of the procedures described in the homebrew literature to create your own toasted malt that will contribute character to your finished product.

Another option you might try is to use some of the new specialty malts that are showing up in homebrew shops now under names like victory malt or special roast. Used in small quantities, these malts will help to add character and complexity without stepping to the front of the flavor profile.

Wheat Malt

This is another idiosyncratic ingredient in bock recipes. Only two of the recipes I examined used wheat, but both were AHA winners and both used a significant amount of wheat—5 to 10 percent of the total mash. Judges' comments on one of them consistently mentioned good head retention, which likely was assisted by the wheat.

Mash Procedures

Once the grain brewers assemble their grist, it's time to mash. Traditional German brewing calls for a decoction mash to achieve the ideal finished beer. If you want to try decoction, see Greg Noonan's (1986) excellent book *Brewing Lager Beer* for a full discussion of how it's done. Few homebrewers, however, use this technique. All of the recipes I examined relied on a multi-step infusion mash.

While mash schedules are highly variable, I did notice a few trends in the recipes. First, virtually all of the mashes used a protein rest somewhere in the 120 to 135 degree F (49 to 57 degree C) range. Starch conversion often included a rest in the 146 to 150 degree F (63.5 to 66.5 degree C) range and/or a rest in the 156 to 160 degree F (69 to 71 degree C) range.

In addition to looking at recipes, I recently read an article by Bruce Brode (1992) of the Maltose Falcons on the subject of bock mashes. He notes that there are two schools of thought about the saccharification rest for a bock mash. One school says it should be 158 to 160 degrees F (70 to 72.5 degrees C), the other aims for the 145 to 153 degree F (62.5 to 67 degree C) range. Brode argues for the lower temperature range in order to produce plenty of fermentable sugars and achieve the desired alcohol level for the style, and he notes that high-kilned malts—if extensively used—will adequately dextrinize the wort.

We already know that there are two schools of thought concerning which base malt is best for making a bock—Munich or lager malt. It would make sense to mash a Munich-based grist at 150 degrees F (66.5 degrees C) or less, while you would want to give the lager malt a rest at 155 degrees F (68 degrees C) or above to generate some dextrins. A quick check of Miller (1988) and Noonan (1986) bears this idea out. Miller, who advocates Munich malt for 85 percent of the grist, suggests a two-hour saccharification rest in the range of 150 to 141 degrees F (65.5 to 60.5 degrees C). Noonan, whose recipe calls for twice as much lager malt as Munich, recommends a rest at 155 degrees F (68 degrees C).

The key to bock mashing, then, lies in the choices made in assembling the grist. Those who use a predominantly Munich-based approach should mash at lower saccharification temperatures and let the ingredients do their work. Those who are following the lager malt approach should plan to include a dextrin-level rest.

HOPS: ACHIEVING A CAREFUL BALANCE

The use of hops in a bock beer must be very delicate. The style descriptions for bock and doppelbock call for low hop character on all counts: bitterness, flavor and aroma. In formulating a bock, you want to add only enough hops to provide some balance to the malt and prevent it from becoming cloying. The best way to find the right balance is to calculate your hop additions in terms of international bitterness units (IBUs). Figure 5 provides some general guidelines for converting homebrew bittering units (HBUs) to IBUs when making a bock. If you have begun to formulate your own recipes, you should be working with IBUs—check out Jackie Rager's article in the 1990 special issue of *zymurgy* (see his Table 1, pp. 53-54), for a full discussion of how this is done.

The various style descriptions for bock call for 20 to 30 IBUs. For a traditional bock with a gravity of about 1.068, this equates to between 6.5 and 10 HBUs of hops boiled for 45 minutes.

When it comes to Doppelbocks, there is a bit more disagreement about the appropriate hop levels. Some authorities say that Doppelbocks can be hopped at levels up to 40 IBUs, yet none of the commercial examples for which we have data indicate hop levels beyond 30 IBUs. The latest guidelines from the Association of Brewers, published in the March-April 1992 issue of *The New Brewer*, give a range from 17 to 27

FIGURE 5

IBU to HBU Conversions for Bock Beers

For a beer with the specific gravity indicated, the number of IBUs shown in the left column can be achieved using a 45 minute boil with the HBUs shown in the right column.

Bock		Doppelbock	
SG: 1.066		SG: 1.075	
FG: 1.074		FG: 1.082	
IBUs	HBUs	IBUs	HBUs
20	6.5	18	6.1
22	7.2	20	6.8
24	7.8	22	7.5
26	7.8	24	8.2
28	8.5	26	8.9
30	9.75	28	9.6
		30	10.2
		35	12.0

IBUs, which may more closely resemble current commercial practice. For those of you who want to explore either end of the spectrum, Figure 5 provides HBU conversions for IBU levels ranging from 18 to 35 in a 1.075 wort.

Hop Additions

Many bock recipes call for only one hop addition 30 to 45 minutes before the end of the boil. This type of hop schedule allows you to meet the strict characteristics of the style. Still,

FIGURE 6
Hop Additions by Recipe

RECIPE	Minutes Boiled				Steep or Dry Hop
	60	30-45	15	5	
1	H				
7	C & StG				
12	CH	H & T	T		
11	W	W			T
21	H				H
20	B		F		S
5	Sp	T		H	
2	H			H	
3	P			H	T
4	P			H	T
6	T & H			H	T
10	H	H		H	H
TOTALS	14	5	2	6	7

H = Hallertauer, T = Tettnanger, P = Perle, Sp = Spaltz

C = Cascade, StG = Styrian Goldings, Ch = Chinook, B = Bullion

F = Fuggles, S = Saaz, W = Willamette

many of the successful recipes that I examined also used some late hop additions. Figure 6 shows the timing of these additions. As you can see, it is difficult to draw many conclusions from these data about the best way to handle late hop additions in a bock—many different patterns appear to have been successful.

All the late additions, however, were of small quantities of hops, generally one-quarter to one-half ounce. The size of these additions allowed the hops to provide some additional balance and complexity without becoming noticeable enough to take the beer out of category. So if you do add hops near the end of the boil, go easy on the quantity.

Hop Selection

Hallertauer is the hop of choice for bocks. Among the recipes that I examined, 75 percent used Hallertauer at least once, and this hop accounted for 43 percent of all hop additions. Tettnanger was the number two preference, accounting for 24 percent of all hop additions. See Figure 7 for a breakdown of hop selection by variety.

Figure 6 also shows when each hop type was used. You'll notice that for late hop additions Hallertauer and Tettnanger were heavily favored. Together they account for more than 80

FIGURE 7
Hop Varieties Used

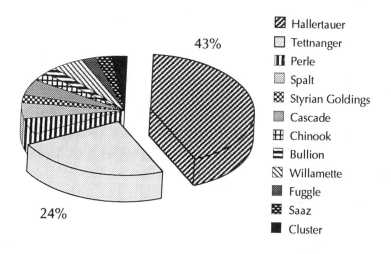

43%

24%

- ▨ Hallertauer
- ☐ Tettnanger
- ▮▮ Perle
- ▨ Spalt
- ▩ Styrian Goldings
- ▨ Cascade
- ⊞ Chinook
- ▤ Bullion
- ▨ Willamette
- ▨ Fuggle
- ▨ Saaz
- ▪ Cluster

percent of all hops boiled less than 60 minutes, and nearly 90 percent of the hops added within the last 15 minutes of the boil. This pattern of hop selection is clearly characteristic of the style and should be closely followed if you want to make an authentic bock.

As a starting point, I recommend a hop schedule that calls for Hallertauer boiling hops 45 minutes before the end of the boil and a small addition of Hallertauer near the end of the boil or as a post-boil steep. It is hard to go wrong with this plan—the beer you make will be in style in all aspects of hop character. If you decide you want to experiment from there, at least you'll know what your starting point is.

YEAST AND FERMENTATION

Like most of the well-known German beer styles, bocks are made using bottom-fermenting lager yeast. To brew a bock with the proper characteristics, you will need to ferment at lager temperatures—usually between 45 and 55 degrees F (7 and 13 degrees C). Furthermore, these high-gravity beers benefit substantially from long periods of lagering at temperatures near freezing. Let's look at the fermentation of a bock beer.

First you'll have to decide on yeast. The winning recipes that I reviewed used a broad variety of yeasts. Liquid yeasts were used in 60 percent of the brews, dry yeasts in the other 40 percent. I was surprised at the high proportion of dry yeasts, but it may be due to the fact that some of the recipes pre-date the widespread availability of good liquid yeast cultures. Today, it is hard for me to imagine investing the effort and especially the *time* that it takes to make a good lager without using the best yeast you can get—and that usually means a liquid culture.

I am in the process of brewing some bocks with the Wyeast Pilsen and Bohemian lager yeasts (Nos. 2007 and 2124 respectively), but I can't yet recommend them for bocks. The best candidate for bock-making is Wyeast No. 2206, the Bavarian Lager yeast. Byron Burch recommended it recently in one of his newsletters, and I have been happy with it in my own efforts. The accent is on maltiness and complexity and it gives you a rich, full-bodied beer. Flocculation is medium and apparent attenuation is 73 to 77 percent. Optimal fermentation temperature is 48 degrees F (9 degrees C).

By the way, if you are tempted to try Wyeast No. 2308 Munich yeast, I would advise against it. This yeast has been around awhile and some people have made good beer with it, but it is a bit finicky and requires several different fermentation temperatures to achieve optimal results.

When fermenting at the recommended temperature for lager yeasts, the primary fermentation can take several weeks. When planning my brews, I usually count on a month at the optimal fermentation temperature before I can lower the temperature and begin lagering. I usually rack from primary to secondary after two to three weeks, then drop the temperature in the refrigerator once visible fermentation activity has ceased. If there is more than a fine layer of yeast at the bottom of the carboy when I begin lagering, I'll usually try to rack again to prevent any off-flavors from yeast autolysis.

Commercial breweries get away with three weeks of lagering for most of their top-fermented beers, but good bocks take more time and care. Traditionally, bocks were made on the first day of fall to be served in the spring. During the long German winter, they lagered in cold caves. Salvator, the original Doppelbock, is still made today in Germany, and is lagered for a full two-and-a-half months. You should keep these traditions in mind when brewing your own bock and try for the longest lagering period that you can stand. Also, the bigger your bock gets, the longer it should lager. Just as high-gravity ales take time to mellow and age, so do these high-gravity lagers. Give them some time and you will be happy with the results.

If you are short on refrigerator space, but you live in a part of the country that has long winters, you might get away with ambient temperature lagering outdoors or in your garage. Pack the carboy away with some vodka in the air lock and forget about it until the temperature warms up again.

CONCLUSION

After all this discussion, you might wonder if you're ever going to be able to wade through all the options and actually get down to brewing a bock. Let me give you a quick summary of the ingredients I would use if I were going to brew a bock today.

As we have seen, good extract bocks are certainly possible and, for many brewers, using extract is a very practical way to achieve the desired gravity. But regardless of whether you are going to use extract or try an all-grain approach, I recommend that you do a mash or mini-mash that includes (for a 5-gallon batch):

Grain	Mini-Mash	Full Mash
Munich malt	2 pounds (908 g)	Up to 10 pounds (4.5 kg)
Dark crystal malt	1 pound (454 g)	Up to 3 pounds (1.4 kg)
Chocolate malt	4 ounces (113 g)	Up to 8 ounces (226 g)
Other/toasted malts	4 ounces (113 g)	Up to 1 pound total (454 g)

Once you have this basic grain bill together, you can add enough extract or two-row lager malt to bring the expected gravity up to your target level. You will want some two-row in the mini-mash as well for the additional enzyme power.

Hop with enough Hallertauer added 45 minutes before the end of the boil to reach an IBU level in the proper range, then throw in another quarter ounce sometime in the last 15 minutes of the boil just for a hint of hop flavor.

Ferment at 48 degrees F (9 degrees C) with Wyeast No. 2206 Bavarian Lager yeast. When visible fermentation is complete find a cold (33 degree F [0.5 degree C]) refrigerator and lock your creation away for at least three—and preferably eight or 10—weeks.

An official Chicago Beer Society "Beer Geek," Ray Daniels has been homebrewing since 1989, and collecting honors in both national and regional competitions since 1990. He applies his training in biochemistry to the study and production of lager beers, and he is co-holder of the 1991 Midwest Brewer of the Year title.

APPENDIX
Recipes Included in Analysis

Recipe No.	Brewer / Beer name Source

1. Darryl Richman, "Bock Aasswards"
    Winner's circle (1990). *zymurgy* 13:4 , pp. 65-66.

2. Ronald Brubacker, "Stimulator"
    Winner's circle (1989). *zymurgy* 12:4, p. 67.

3. Gregory Noonan, Maibock
    Noonan, G. (1986). *Brewing Lager Beer.* Boulder, Colo.: Brewers
    Publications, pp. 183-184.

4. Gregory Noonan, Doppelbock
    Brewing Lager Beer, p. 184.

5. Byron Burch, "Billygoat's Downfall Bock"
    Burch, B. (Fall, 1990). Salute to 1990: Recipes and commentary.
    The Beverage People News, p. 5. (Available from Great Fermenta-
    tions, Santa Rosa, Calif.)

6. John Judd and Don Hoag, "Hansbock"
    American Homebrewers Association (Ed.) (1989). *Winners Circle.*
    Boulder, Colo.: Brewers Publications, pp. 122-123.

7. J. C. Martin, C. C. Martin, and C. R. Grimes, "Old Fort Worth
    Bock"
    Winner's Circle, pp. 123-124.

8. Dave Miller, bock, all-grain recipe
    Miller, D. (1988). *The Complete Handbook of Home Brewing.* Pownal,
    Vt.: Storey Communications, p. 209.

9. Dave Miller, American bock, all-grain recipe
    The Complete Handbook of Home Brewing, p. 211.

10. Keith Wilbourn, "Tracey's First"
    Winners Circle, p. 120.

11. Gary W. Schmidt, "Ehren Bock"
     Winners Circle, pp. 121-122.

12. Tom Ayres, "Bock-in-the-Saddle (Again)."
     Winners Circle, pp. 119-120.

13. Charlie Papazian, "Borborygmous Bock"
     Papazian, C. (1984). *The Complete Joy of Home Brewing.* New
     York: Avon Books, pp. 174-175.

14. Charlie Papazian, "Danger Knows No Favorites Bock"
     The Complete Joy of Home Brewing, pp. 175-176.

15. Charlie Papazian, "Purple Mountain Bock"
     The Complete Joy of Home Brewing, pp. 176-177.

16. Dave Miller, Bock, partial mash
     The Complete Handbook of Home Brewing, p. 209.

17. Dave Miller, Doppelbock
     The Complete Handbook of Home Brewing, p. 210.

18. Dave Miller, Doppelbock, partial mash recipe
     The Complete Handbook of Home Brewing, p. 210.

19. Dave Miller, American bock, partial mash recipe
     The Complete Handbook of Home Brewing, p. 211.

20. Steve Crossan, "Doppelbock"
     Winners Circle, pp. 124-125.

21. Lt. Col. Charles F. Smith, "Konsumator"
     Winners Circle, pp. 125-126.

22. Byron Burch, Bock
     Burch, B. (1986). *Brewing Quality Beers.* Fulton, Calif.: Joby
     Books, p. 54.

23. Byron Burch, Dopplebock
     Brewing Quality Beers, p. 55.

REFERENCES

Brode, B. L. (April, 1992). Bock to the future. *Brews & News*, 12-14. (Newsletter of the Maltose Falcons.)

Burch, B. (1986). *Brewing Quality Beers*. Fulton, Calif.: Joby Books.

Burch, B. (1989). Of yeasts and beer styles. *zymurgy*, 12:4., 55-63.

Eckhardt, F. (1989). *The Essentials of Beer Style*. Portland, Ore.: Fred Eckhardt Associates.

Jackson, M. (1988). *The New World Guide to Beer*. Philadelphia: Running Press Book Publishers.

Krus, D. L. (Oct. 17, 1991). Yeast and specific gravities. *Internet Hombrew Digest*, No. 742.

Miller, D. (1988). *The Complete Handbook of Home Brewing*. Pownal, Vt.: Storey Communications, Inc.

Noonan, G. J. (1986). *Brewing Lager Beer*. Boulder, Colo.: Brewers Publications.

Rager, J. (1990). Calculating hop bitterness in beer. *zymurgy*, 13:4, 53-54.

15. Evaluation of Pitching Yeast

George Fix
Author, Principles of Brewing Science

The last few years have seen remarkable advances in the general area of yeast evaluation for small-scale brewers. Most of this work has been motivated by the needs of the growing number of brewpubs that are cropping up all over North America. A lot of these results, if not all of them, are useful to serious homebrewers as well. The goal of this article is to survey those which seem to have greatest relevance.

One important caveat should be noted. It is assumed that these tests will be used in the kind of environment found in most homebrewing and brewpub situations; that is, the beer will be in good and loving hands from the start of brewing to the time it is consumed. If I were going to be held responsible for the stability and quality of unpasteurized beer that is packaged in itsy-bitsy 12-ounce bottles and is required to stand up to abuse in trade conditions for months, then I

George Fix

would have to recommend different evaluation methods. They would be more sophisticated and considerably more expensive. However, the real value of the hands-on practical experience that has been gained over the last four or five years is that, for brewpubs and homebrewers, simpler and cheaper methods are perfectly adequate.

Suppose now that we are sitting at a desk planning our next brew, which is to be done in a few days. Suppose we have available either a glass carboy containing yeast and a cover solution (beer and/or wort), or a stainless-steel canister with the same contents. The carboy looks like a starter, possibly from liquid yeast, yeast brought up from slants, or a starter made from dried yeast. The yeast in the canister looks as if it were collected from a previous fermentation. While the origin of yeast and yeast management are issues that we will ultimately have to deal with in an article like this, the relevant question at this point is the role this yeast solution will play in our next brew, quite apart of its origin. In this regard the following four possible scenarios are envisioned:

SCENARIO NO. 1: GO WITH IT

In this scenario we are satisfied with the type of beer the yeast is capable of brewing. We also feel comfortable that bacterial and wild yeast counts are sufficiently low so problems will not arise with these contaminants. Finally, we are satisfied with the viability of the yeast, so on brew day the only task is to decant off the cover solution and measure out the right amount of yeast for pitching. Most ale yeast strains are pitched at a rate of 5 to 10 million cells per ml (the higher the starting gravity, the higher the pitching rate). This works out to 1.25 to 2.5 g/L (1/6 to 1/3 ounce/gallon) of wet yeast slurry. Lager strains are usually pitched at 10 to 15 million cells per ml, which amounts to 2.5 to 3.0 g/L (1/3 to 1/2 ounce/gallon) of wet yeast slurry.

SCENARIO NO. 2: DUMP IT

In this scenario we are seriously concerned about one or more of the points raised above. As a consequence we discard the yeast and seek an alternate source.

SCENARIO NO. 3: WORT CHARGE

In this scenario the only point of concern is the viability of the yeast. In such circumstances the addition of sterile wort to the stored yeast may be just what is needed. Practical experience has shown that the optimal time to pitch is when the yeast has just completed its aerobic growth stage, since this is when there is a maximal amount of metabolic energy and overall viability. In fact, Micah Millspaw has devised an interesting and practical scheme for yeast propagation where the aerobic stage takes place entirely in the starter. The main fermentation is entirely anaerobic—not only is the chilled wort not aerated, but the fermenters are filled with carbon dioxide to insure anaerobic conditions. Micah and Bob Jones are preparing an article on their work, and brewers should study their procedures, because they are highly effective.

There is a downside to wort charges, however. As Paul Farnsworth (1989) has correctly pointed out, if there is one place where we are likely to have problems with our yeast work, wort charges are a prime candidate. In fact, there is an old brewer's rule that the less we handle yeast the better. Problems can be avoided in wort charges by being very careful (sterilizing the necks of vessels, pasteurizing the wort used, etc.), but if the charge is not needed, we would be best advised to avoid it. Before we can decide whether or not to use a yeast charge, then, we need information about the viability of the yeast to be pitched.

SCENARIO NO. 4: WASH THE YEAST

In this scenario our concerns focus on bacterial levels in the yeast slurry, and the possibility that they could affect finished beer flavors. Rather than discard the slurry, brewers have sometimes used a yeast wash to deal with this problem. There are a number of desirable features associated with an acid wash of yeast. For example, it has been established that gram-negative bacteria found in pitching yeast (most notably, obesumbacteria, which are sometimes called flavobacteria) will almost always be totally eradicated in a yeast wash. This procedure will also dramatically lower the number of viable gram-positive rods (*Lactobacillus*). Finally, one will typically get a wash in the literal sense, in that residual trub and other organic matter will be scrubbed out. This usually gives a cleaner finish to beer flavors.

The downside to washing yeast is that it is a highly effective way of propagating wild yeast. This is particularly true of so-called wine yeasts (elliptically shaped *Saccharomyces* strains), which are a common source of infection. These strains do much better in an acid wash than culture yeast, and can gain dominance in a slurry that is repeatedly washed over a number of generations. The same is true of a large number of gram-positive cocci (*Pediococcus*). Of course, if the pedios and/or wild yeast are not present, then an acid wash might be just the thing to do. In other circumstances, the best course of action is Scenario No. 2; i.e., dump and look for an alternate source of yeast.

The most effective tool brewers have in sorting through the above options is their own palates, particularly when pitching yeast is reused, for often advance warning can be obtained before a yeast crop becomes dysfunctional in one of the senses cited above. There are other times when the effects are subtle and hard to interpret, however, and in these situations, tasting alone will not be sufficient. In addition, other techniques are obviously needed for the evaluation of new unpitched yeast. The following test procedures were developed for these cases:

1. Detection of gram-positive bacteria (*Pediococcus*, *Lactobacillus*).

2. Detection of gram-negative bacteria (coliforms, obesumbacteria or flavobacteria, pectinates).

3. Estimation of yeast viability.

4. Detection of mutated yeast.

TEST 1: GRAM-POSITIVE BACTERIA

The infection of pitching yeast by anaerobic, acid-forming, gram-positive rods (lactos) and cocci (pedios) is the most common yeast disorder. Thus, their detection is at the top of our priority list. The most common sources of infection are the following:

(i) Bacteria were originally present in the purchased yeast. This is very common with mass-produced dry yeast (see Farnsworth, 1989).

(ii) If a yeast slurry that is stored between brews goes dormant, then low and insignificant levels of infection can grow and become problematic. This can be avoided by storing yeast with sterile wort at low temperatures and, of course, keeping the length of the storage period to a minimum.

(iii) In some brewing environments airborne particulate matter (especially malt dust) will contain gram positives and other bacteria relevant to beer. This will be a problem for brewers only if unclean conditions prevail; i.e., if the brewing equipment has residual organic material in it.

Lactos and pedios produce lactic acid, which, at levels above its flavor threshold, will always impart an unmistakable acidic, sour character. Diacetyl may also be produced by these bacteria. Many mechanisms lead to the presence of diacetyl in the finished beer, but the diacetyl formed by the gram positives has a raunchy (rancid butter) character that is easy to detect.

The procedure recommended for detection of gram-positive bacteria is based on Hsu's Lactobacillus Pediococcus medium (HLP), available from J.E. Siebel Sons' Co. in Chicago. The reader is warned that this is a crude medium, primarily because it contains sulfates (see Figure 1) to create anaerobic conditions. The latter is essential for the detection of lactos and pedios. Because sulfuric acid is partially harmful to bacteria, the procedure will always undercount the number of bacteria present. Nevertheless, if sampling is done in the proper way, the presence of gram positives can be detected at levels below what is needed for the flavor of the fermented beer to be affected. The big advantage of this medium is that it is "user friendly" in the extreme.

Readers should also consult Teri Fahrendorf's (1990) excellent article on HLP. The media from Siebel also comes with complete instructions.

FIGURE 1

Chemical Identity, Hsu's Lactobacillus Pediococcus Medium*

Agar	2%
Sodium acetate	4%
Tomato juice broth	29%
Malt extract	7%
Peptone	7%
Calcium pantothenate	1%
Citric acid	2%
Dextrin	0.1%
Sodium sulfate	2%
Sodium thioglycolate	1%
Cycloheximide	0.01%

* From J.E. Siebel Sons' Co., Inc., HLP Medium Material Safety Data Sheet.

Materials Needed

HLP, 16-x-150-mm test tubes, pipettes, water bath capable of maintaining 85 degrees F (30 degrees C), syringe (see Figure 2).

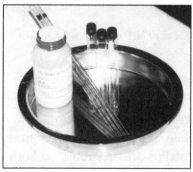

Figure 2. Materials for Test No. 1.

Preparation of Medium

Use 7 grams of HLP per 100 ml of water. Each test tube should contain 25 ml of dissolved medium, so we'll have 4 tubes per 100 ml water. The tubes will keep if refrigerated, so it is often convenient to prepare many tubes at one time. Distilled water is preferred over normal tap water. Specific steps are listed below:

(i) Sterilize test tubes and syringe.

(ii) Bring water to a boil.

(iii) Stir in HLP powder and hold at a boil for 3 minutes.

(iv) Remove from heat, and add 25 ml of medium to test tubes with syringe.

(v) Store tubes in a refrigerator. (See Figure 3).

Figure 3. Tubes of HLP stored in refrigerator.

Where to Sample

The key to getting reasonable results is to draw samples from locations where the bacteria are most likely to be found. Both lactos and pedios are anaerobic, so both are generally located near the bottom of the vessels. In particular, they favor the top of the yeast layer at the bottom of a fermenter or other container. Specific suggestions for sampling are listed below.

(i) Fermentation end point. Practical experience has shown that the most accurate results with HLP are obtained by sampling just before the fermented beer is transferred to storage. The author's set-up is shown in Figure 4. Here half kegs are used as fermenters, and 5-gallon kegs are used as storage vessels. Fermented beer is pushed out of the fermenter by carbon dioxide pressure into the storage kegs. The first quart or so will be cloudy, consisting of the top yeast sediment layer. It is this liquid that is to be collected for sampling. Obvious modifications are used for siphon systems. The liquid so collected should be refrigerated until a definite yeast layer forms (two to three hours).

Figure 4. The author's set-up.

(ii) Yeast in storage. It is generally advisable to sample yeast that has been stored, particularly if the storage period is longer than seven days. Samples are drawn from the vessels (carboy or canister) in exactly the same way as they are drawn from fermenters.

(iii) Forced fermentation. Here one removes a small amount of wort (about 500 ml), and combines it with a sample of pitching yeast at two to three times the normal rate. An elevated temperature is maintained—68 to 77 degrees F (20 to 25 degrees C) for lagers and 77 to 82 degrees F (25 to 28 degrees C) for ales. Sampling is done as above. One should cool the sample down for 12 to 24 hours to allow for the formation of a bottom yeast sediment before sampling. Also, measuring the gravity at the end of the forced fermentation will give advance notice of what the final gravity of the main batch should be.

Innoculation

I used to do the innoculation inside a transfer box, but experiments showed that this was not necessary. A clean working area will do, although it probably would not hurt to scrub the work area with a lysol solution or the equivalent before innoculation. Siebel's instructions suggest that one should pipette 0.1 to 1.0 ml of sample into the tube. It is my view that a full milliliter (1.0 ml) should be added, which apparently is the maximum amount the medium can support. Specific steps in the innoculation are as follows:

(i) Sterilize the pipettes.

(ii) Heat tubes to be innoculated (two to three per 5 gallons is sufficient) to 176 degrees F (80 degrees C) (Figure 5). Let them cool to 104 degrees F (40 degrees C), which is the temperature at which innoculation should take place.

(iii) Pipette 1 ml of sample into each tube. Try to remove liquid from the top of the yeast layer, but minimize the amount of yeast added (see Figure 6).

Figure 5.   Heating the test tubes of HLP.

Figure 6.   Pipetting wort from just above the yeast layer for transfer to test tubes.

(iv) Invert the tubes a couple of times to dissolve the sample.

(v)   Place tubes in a water bath at 85 degrees F (30 degrees C) for 72 hours. (See Figure 7).

Figure 7.   Test tubes in a water bath.

Analysis

The presence of lactos is indicated by tornadolike strings in the bottom two-thirds of the tube. (Siebel's instructions has pictures, as does Fahrendorf's article). Each tornado structure represents one cell that grew in the tube. Since 1 ml of sample was added, the number of tornado structures gives the number of lactos per ml. Experience has shown that this will undercount by a factor of 10; hence two tornados mean that there were around $2 \times 10 = 20$ lactos per ml in the sample.

Pedios show as oval structures which recall rugby balls. Here, the undercount is typically less than that with lactos; in my experience it is a factor of about five.

Yeast will show up as a cloud throughout the tube. If there is too much yeast carry over, this yeast cloud can obscure the visual identification. Siebel's instructions describe an alternate procedure using membrane filtration that avoids this problem. This alternative also tends to give lower undercounts.

Siebel's instructions suggest that a dense cloud at the top of the tube indicates the presence of aerobic bacteria relevant to beer. It has been my experience that this is not necessarily the case. Virtually anything can be at the top, including aerobics, yeast, and/or microbes not relevant to beer. This is of course a defect common to "artificial" media; i.e., media that are unlike beer. It is for this reason that this procedure should only be used as a test for lactos and pedios.

Criterion

Teri Fahendorf (1990) recommends that the yeast can be used as is (option 1) if nothing shows up in the HLP tubes, and I agree. Note that following this guideline amounts to keeping the lactos at a level below 10 cells per ml or, put differently, less than one lacto per million yeast cells. While this criterion might seem very strict, it must be remembered that undesirable bacterial byproducts; e.g., diacetyl, are detectable at low levels. Thus, only a minute amount of wort constituents are needed to produce them at unacceptable levels. Siebel actually recommends a stricter criterion of at most one bacterial cell per ml.

Yeast in which only a few lactos show up in the tube can be reused if it is washed before pitching. Yeast that shows the presence of pedios should be discarded, totally independent of any other consideration.

TEST 2: GRAM-NEGATIVE BACTERIA

This is the oldest microbiological test still in current use. The object is to see how much (if any) infection is passed on to the fermenter from chilled and aerated wort.

Procedure

Remove approximately 500 ml of chilled and aerated wort just before the yeast is pitched. Hold this sample in a water bath at 85 degrees F (30 degrees C) until instabilities become apparent. This includes the formation of haze, gas production or any other hints of metabolic activity.

It is relatively easy to identify the type of microbes that are present. Traditionally, this procedure has been called the "sniff and snort test," because the aroma of the sample after it goes unstable will usually indicate the cause of the instability. Gram negatives are usually big sulfur producers. Their presence is indicated by a strong cornlike smell that also may recall rotten vegetables and/or parsnip. An acidic/bacterial smell usually means that thermophilic lactic acid bacteria (most likely *Lactobacillus delbrueckii*) are present.

If you have doubts about what microbes are present, then the following simple equivalent of a gram stain can be used. Use a sterile loop to place a part of the sediment on a sterile glass surface. With a separate sterile loop add a 3 percent aqueous solution of potassium hydroxide (KOH). Gram-negative microbes become viscous when mixed with KOH, while gram-positive bacteria will not react.

Criteria

The following are the traditional guidelines associated with the water bath procedure:

Length of Stable Period	Comments
24 hours	This represents a serious wort infection. Finished beer flavors will likely be affected.
24 to 48 hours	This is a less serious situation, although still unacceptable. Finished beer will be affected perhaps only in subtle ways.
48 to 72 hours	Finished beer will not be affected, although someone is not doing a very inspiring job vis-à-vis sanitation.
72 hours	The desirable situation.

TEST 3: YEAST VIABILITY

Staining techniques have long been used to estimate the percentage of viable yeast cells. Currently, the ASBC (1976) recommends methylene blue. However, Rodney Morris has pointed out that this stain may give errors up to 40 percent. Rodney recommends Rhodamine B, whose error is typically below 10 percent. He formulated the procedure and dye described below.

Materials Needed

Rhodamine B (Fisher Scientific or Kodak), NaOH, phenol alcohol (Kodak), citric acid, microscope, pH meter, filter.

Preparation of Dye

Prepare a 1 percent weight to volume solution of citric acid in distilled water. Adjust pH to 6.0 with NaOH. Use this buffer to make a 0.2 percent solution of Rhodamine B. Add a few drops of phenol alcohol to inhibit bacterial growth, and filter. (A coffee filter paper will work in a pinch, but don't tell Rodney I said this!)

Procedure

To test for yeast viability, mix two drops of yeast sediment with one drop of Rhodamine B. Add a coverslip and examine at 200x to 400x with a microscope. Non-viable yeast cells stain red. Various bacteria stain pink-red, but they will be detectable only at very high levels of infection and with magnifications of 1000x with oil immersion.

Criterion

The standard rule in large-scale brewing is not to pitch yeast which is less than 90 percent viable; i.e., if more than 10 percent of the cells in the test stain red. Small-scale brewers are often less exacting in their requirements, if they do the test at all. Failure to check yeast viability sometimes leads to underpitching the required amount of viable cells, which in turn can sometimes lead to less than ideal ferments. While individual brewers will want to develop their own criteria, my rules are the following: ale yeast below 67 percent viability should not be repitched, and the concentration of viable cells should fall in the 5 to 10 million cells per ml range. With lager yeast, these numbers are increased to 75 percent, and 10 to 15 million cells per ml, respectively.

TEST 4: YEAST MUTATION

Mutated yeast are best classified in terms of their functional disorders. The following are the most common:
(i)   Loss of flocculation.
(ii) Loss of the ability to ferment sugars like maltotriose.
(iii) Respiratory deficiencies.

Loss of the ability to properly flocculate is not uncommon. Usually mutants of this type are normal in other respects. For example, the three-strain Whitbread culture has two nonflocculate fermenters, which are mutants, from a technical point of view. Fortunately, the third strain, a nonfermenting flocculator, is capable of mechanically removing yeast at the end point of fermentation. Many nonflocculant yeast strains actually display superior fermentation characteristics, most notably in the reduction of byproducts like diacetyl. Molsen's maintains a yeast culture of this type—it remains in suspension throughout the fermentation, and then is removed via a centrifuge. The major problem with using nonflocculant yeast is that extraordinary measures are needed to clarify the fermented beer.

The loss of fermentation power is also common, and is generally a more serious problem. Residual fermentable sugars serve as excellent carbon sources for a variety of bacteria. Moreover, even if bacterial activity does not occur, the beer's balance and overall flavor profile typically will be altered in unacceptable ways.

Both of these defects can be readily detected in a forced fermentation using either production wort or wort specially prepared for this check. The loss of flocculation can be identified by direct examination at the end of the cooling period.

Specially prepared wort is recommended to check fermentation characteristics. A good choice is an all-malt wort with an original extract (OE) of 12 °Plato (1.048) that is 65 percent fermentable. This can be achieved by a single-temperature infusion mash at 154 degrees F (68 degrees C). With normal yeast the amount of residual extract left at the end of the fermentation (i.e., the real extract RE) is the following:

$$RE = 12 \times (1 - 65/100)$$
$$= 12 \times .35$$
$$= 4.2 \,°Plato.$$

The measured extract (i.e., apparent extract AE) is well approximated by the following formula:

$$AE = (RE - .1808 \times OE) / .8192$$
$$= (4.2 - .1808 \times 12) / .8192$$
$$= 2.5 \,°Plato$$
(which is equivalent to a specific gravity of 1.010).

In the case of serious mutation, all maltotriose (typically 18 percent of the total original extract) and some maltose is not fermented. As a consequence, something like 45 percent of the original extract is fermented instead of 65 percent. Thus, the real extract is

$$RE = 12 \times (1 - 45 / 100)$$
$$= 12 \times .65$$
$$= 7.8$$

and the measured extract is

$$AE = (7.8 - .1808 \times 12) / .8192$$
$$= 6.9 \; °Plato$$

This means that the final gravity is 1.027 instead of 1.010.

The situation with respiratory deficient (RD) yeast is even more serious, primarily because these mutants are capable of generating elevated levels of diacetyl and fusel alcohols, to cite only two defects. The test for RD mutants is the most elaborate in this article, but no more difficult to carry out than the others. This procedure considerably simplifies the one recommended by the ASBC (1976), and I am grateful to Rodney Morris for developing it.

Materials Needed

MYGP medium (Difco), triphenyl tetrazolium red, .06 M potassium phosphate buffer (pH = 7.0), filter membrane, petri dishes, forceps, microscope (200x).

Procedure

(i) Prepare a stock solution containing 0.1 percent triphenyl tetrazolium red in .06 M potassium phosphate buffer. This stock can be stored in brown bottles in a freezer.

(ii) Start the test by growing yeast in a petri dish on a filter membrane with the MYGP medium until a colony size of 1 to 2 mm diameter is achieved.

(iii) Use the forceps to transfer the filter membrane to a new petri dish. Saturate with tetrazolium red stock solution.

(iv) Within a few minutes normal yeast cells will start staining red, and this process will continue over a two to four hour period. RD mutants remain unstained.

Criterion

It is my opinion that if the level of RD mutants is below 1 percent, finished beer flavors will not be affected. Serious flavor disorders occur when RD mutants account for 10 to 20 percent of the total (or more).

George Fix, a native Texan, lives with his wife Laurie in Arlington. George earned his doctorate from Harvard University and has been on the faculty at Harvard, the University of Michigan and Carnegie-Mellon University. Currently, he is chairman of the department of mathematics at the University of Texas at Arlington and is also the senior consultant for Brewers Research and Development Company. George has won 60 brewing awards, including two best-of-shows in AHA- and HWBTA-sanctioned competitions.

REFERENCES

ASBC (1976). *Methods of Analysis*, 7th edition. Milwaukee, Wis.: ASBC.
Fahrendorf, T. (1990). Building an incubator and home lab culturing. In *Beer and Brewing, Vol. 10*, pp. 155-176. Boulder, Colo.: Brewers Publications.
Farnsworth, P. (1989). Healthy homebrew starter cultures. *zymurgy*, 12:4., 10-13.

THE AMERICAN HOMEBREWERS ASSOCIATION'S
MAGAZINE FOR HOMEBREWERS AND BEER LOVERS

Join the Thousands of Homebrewers Who Read *zymurgy*

Learn What's New in Homebrewing Including:

- New Recipes • Product Reviews • Tips for Beginners • Beer News
- New Brewing Techniques • Equipment and Ingredients
- Beer History • And Much, Much More!

SATISFACTION GUARANTEED!

Published five times a year by the American Homebrewers Association, *zymurgy* is included with membership.

Mail this coupon today! Or call now for credit card order at (303) 447-0816, FAX (303) 447-2825.

_____ENCLOSED IS $25 FOR ONE FULL YEAR
(CANADIAN/FOREIGN MEMBERSHIPS ARE $30 US)
_____PLEASE CHARGE MY CREDIT CARD □ VISA □ MC

CARD NO._____ EXP. DATE_____

SIGNATURE _____

NAME _____

ADDRESS _____

CITY_____ STATE/PROVINCE_____

ZIP/POSTAL CODE _____ COUNTRY_____

PHONE _____

Make check to: American Homebrewers Association, PO Box 1510, Boulder, CO 80306 USA
Offer valid until 12-31-93.

BB12BP

Examine the World of Microbrewing and Pubbrewing

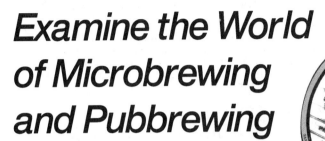

Travel the world of commercial, small-scale brewing; the realm of microbrewers and pub-brewers.

The New Brewer magazine guides you through this new industry. Its pages introduce you to marketing, finance, operations, equipment, recipes, interviews—in short, the whole landscape.

Subscribe to *The New Brewer* and become a seasoned traveler.

Books for your Brewing Library. . .
from Brewers Publications

All prices are quoted in U.S. dollars. Prices may change and shipping charges vary. Brewers Publications is a division of the Association of Brewers. Other divisions are the American Homebrewers Association, the Institute for Brewing Studies and the Great American Beer Festival. For information, write or call: Brewers Publications, PO Box 1679, Boulder, CO 80306-1679 USA. Telephone (303) 447-0816, FAX (303) 447-2825.

Dictionary of Beer and Brewing

This valuable reference will make an outstanding contribution to any brewing library! Author Carl Forget has compiled 1,929 essential definitions used in beermaking, including: Brewing Processes • Ingredients • Types and Styles of Beer • Abbreviations • Arcane Terms • Also: Conversion Tables for temperatures, alcohol percentages and factors.

6 x 9, 186 pp.   **Suggested retail price $19.95**

Brewing Lager Beer

This classic reference book is a must for serious brewers interested in all-grain brewing and recipes. First, author Greg Noonan describes the brewing process and ingredients in plain English. Then he guides you through planning and brewing seven classic lager beers — including recipes. As a bonus, the tables of brewing information are excellent.

5 1/2 x 8 1/2, 320 pp. 4th Printing.   **Suggested retail price $14.95**

Brewing Mead

Mead is a wonderful honey wine with great, untapped commercial value. Charlie Papazian gives step-by-step recipes and instructions for making several varieties of this honey-based brew. Mead was the beverage of royalty in Europe and was reportedly a powerful aphrodisiac. Lt. Col. Robert Gayre of Scotland gives its history. Now is the time to discover the exotic secrets of mead.

5 1/2 x 8 1/2, 200 pp. 2nd Printing.   **Suggested retail price $11.95**

Beer and Brewing, Vol. 8

Transcript of the 1988 Conference on Quality Beer and Brewing

There's a world of beer in this transcript, from practical brewing techniques to a perspective of beers abroad given by European brewers. Chapters include: Improved Record-Keeping • Practical All-Grain Brewing • Aroma ID Kit Development • Making Amazing Mead • Brewpubs in Austria.

5 1/2 x 8 1/2, 220 pp.   **Suggested retail price $21.95**

Beer and Brewing, Vol. 9

Transcript of the 1989 Conference on Quality Beer and Brewing

Here are the transcripts from the biggest AHA Conference ever. This exciting book recaptures the spirit of the event and overflows with invaluable tips in each of its 13 chapters, including: What Makes an Ale an Ale • Clear Beer Please! • Hop Madness • Applying Science to the Art of Brewing.

5 1/2 x 8 1/2, 247 pp.   **Suggested retail price $21.95**

Beer and Brewing, Vol. 10

Transcript of the 1990 Conference on Quality Beer and Brewing

Read all the talks that made four days in Oakland the ultimate homebrew experience. A dozen talks all focused on the quality of beer and beermaking. Chapters include: Beer Blending ala Judy • Slings of Outrageous Fortune • The World of Malt • Carbonating Your Brew • Home Laboratory Culturing.

5 1/2 x 8 1/2, 198 pp.   **Suggested retail price $21.95**

Brew Free or Die! Beer and Brewing, Vol. 11

Transcript of the 1991 Conference on Quality Beer and Brewing

Brew Free or Die! Beer and Brewing, Vol. 11 gives the homebrewer a wealth of knowledge about brewing, from techniques to recipes, gadgets, computerization and much more. Find out what the experts shared at the 1991 AHA Homebrew Conference in this readable collection of papers. Terry Foster explores pale ale, Greg Noonan counsels on brewing water, Candy Schermerhorn shares her secrets for cooking with beer, and an additional host of experts give their hard-won knowledge in this informative book.

5 1/2 x 8 1/2, 239 pp.   **Suggested retail price $21.95**

Brewery Operations, Vol. 3

1986 Microbrewers Conference Transcript

The Brewery Operations series books provide practical, tried-and-true suggestions for small-scale brewing and marketing. Chapters include: Wort Production • Marketing the Pubbrewery • Contract Brewing • Yeast and Fermentation • Brewery Public Relations • Cottage Brewing.

5 1/2 x 8 1/2, 180 pp.   **Suggested retail price $25.95**

Brewery Operations, Vol. 4

1987 Microbrewers Conference Transcript

Expert information on brewing, marketing, engineering and management. Chapters include: Malt Extract in Microbrewing • Techniques of Major Breweries • Engineering for the Microbrewer • Developing a Marketing Plan • How to Hire Good People • Equipment Systems for the Brewpub • BATF Regulations.

5 1/2 x 8 1/2, 210 pp.   **Suggested retail price $25.95**

Brewery Operations, Vol. 5

1988 Microbrewers Conference Transcript

Are you a brewpub operator, just getting into the industry or thinking of expanding? Then you'll want to know every fact in *Brewery Operations, Vol. 5*. There were 21 specialized presentations (27 speakers in all) at the 1988 Conference, providing practical information for all brewers. Topics include: Brewery Feasibility Studies • Equipment Design Considerations • Franchising •Working with Distributors • Yeast Handling • Product Development • Expanding Your Brewery.

5 1/2 x 8 1/2, 330 pp.   **Suggested retail price $25.95**

Brewery Operations, Vol. 6

1989 Microbrewers Conference Transcript

Your guide to the rapidly changing environment of pub- and microbreweries. Chapters include: Legislative Initiatives • Handling Regulatory Authorities • Beer Packaging Design • Working with Distributors • Quality Assurance Systems • Current Federal Regulations • Offering Other's Beers.

5 1/2 x 8 1/2, 205 pp.   **Suggested retail price $25.95**

Brewery Operations, Vol. 7

1990 Microbrewers Conference Transcript

Brewery Operations, Vol. 7, the transcripts of the Denver Conference for microbrewers and pubbrewers, reviews the world of the new commercial brewer. Subjects in the published transcripts include Jeff Mendel's industry overview; Charlie Papazian's presentation on off-flavors; Fred Scheer, of Frankenmuth Brewery, on bottling; Dan Gordon, of Gordon Biersch Brewpub, on trub; Al Geitner, of Pub Brewing Co., on alternative beverages for the brewpub; John Foley, of Connecticut Brewing Co., on strategic plan for contract brewers and Dan Carey, of J.V. Northwest, on microbrewery design performance.

5 1/2 x 8 1/2, 212 pp.   **Suggested retail price $25.95**

Brewing Under Adversity
Brewery Operations, Vol. 8

1991 Microbrewers Conference Transcripts

It is more difficult than ever to run a successful brewing business in today's climate of anti-alcohol sentiment and restrictive legislation. The 1991 Microbrewers Conference, titled "Brewing Under Adversity," addressed this topic and many others pertaining to the smaller brewing venture, and *Brewing Under Adversity, Brewery Operations, Vol, 8* brings this information to you. Topics include: Brewing Under Adversity, Industry Overview, Packaging for the Environment, Brewpub Design Efficiency and Operating Multiple Units.

5 1/2 x 8 1/2, 246 pp.   **Suggested retail price $25.95**

Brewers Resource Directory

Here are the updated phone numbers, addresses, personnel and descriptions of North American breweries and suppliers you've been waiting for! We know how valuable this publication is by the thousands sold to date. It's the most definitive directory in the industry. You get complete listings for: Microbreweries and Brewpubs • Ingredient Suppliers • Brewing Consultants • Equipment Manufacturers • Large Breweries • Associations and Publications • State Laws and Excise Taxes. Updated and published yearly. Includes a revised and expanded beer styles chapter.

Plus, an informative article and statistics summarizing the year's activities and trends.

8 1/2 x 11, approx. 281 pp.   **Suggested retail price $80.00**

Brewery Planner

A Guide to Opening Your Own Small Brewery

When planning to open a brewery, it only makes sense to find out everything you can from those who have already learned about the business, sometimes the hard way. *Brewery Planner* is designed to prepare the new brewer for every potential obstacle or necessity. It is a collection of articles written by experienced brewers, covering The Physical Plant in Section One, Tips from the Experts in Section Two, Marketing and Distribution in Section Three, and Business Plan, Including Templates for Financial Statements in Section Four. A must for anyone planning to open a brewery.

8 1/2 x 11, 190 pp.   **Suggested retail price $80.00**

The Winners Circle

There is no other book like it! 126 award-winning homebrew recipes for 21 styles of lager, ale and mead.

Start brewing with this refreshing collection of tried-and-true homebrew recipes selected from the winners of the AHA National Homebrew Competition.

5 1/2 x 8 1/2, 196 pp.   **Suggested retail price $11.95**

Principles of Brewing Science

George Fix has created a masterful look at the chemistry and biochemistry of brewing. With a helpful short course in the appendix, this book will unravel the mysteries of brewing, showing you what really goes on during the making of beer and how you can improve it. An absolute must for those who want to get the most out of their brewing.

5 1/2 x 8 1/2, 250 pp.   **Suggested retail price $29.95**

Pale Ale
First in the Classic Beer Style Series

Terry Foster, a British expatriate and renowned expert on British beers has created a technical masterpiece on pale ale, the world's most popular style of ale. Written with an entertaining historical perspective, this book more than measures up to its subject matter.

Chapters include history, character, flavor, ingredients, brewing, methods and comparisons of commercial pale ales.

5 1/2 x 8 1/2, 140 pp.   **Suggested retail price $11.95**

Continental Pilsener
Second in the Classic Beer Style Series

Learn the ingredients and techniques that produce this golden, distinctively hopped lager. Dave Miller, an award-winning brewer and author, takes you through the history, flavor, ingredients and methods of the beer that revolutionized brewing.

You'll also learn about current commercial examples of the style. Professionals and homebrewers alike will enjoy this exploration of a classic beer.

5 1/2 x 8 1/2, 102 pp.   **Suggested retail price $11.95**

Lambic
Third in the Classic Beer Style Series

Lambic, by Jean-Xavier Guinard, is the only book ever published that completely examines this exotic and elusive style. From origins to brewing techniques, *Lambic* unravels the mysteries that make this rare style so popular. *Lambic* contains the only directory of the lambic breweries of Belgium. Guinard, a student of Dr. Michael Lewis at the University of California at Davis, grew up in the shadow of lambic breweries and combined vocation and avocation to produce this wonderful book.

5 1/2 x 8 1/2, 169 pp.   **Suggested retail price $11.95**

Vienna, Märzen, Oktoberfest
Fourth in the Classic Beer Style Series

Vienna, a dark, delicious lager, has never been easier to brew. George Fix, well known homebrewer and beer scientist, and his wife, Laurie, explore the history and techniques of this style, giving recipes and in-depth instructions.

Brewers have long known that this is a difficult beer to make true to style— but *Vienna*, the first book to explore this lager, helps even beginning brewers master it.

5 1/2 x 8/12, 117 pp.   **Suggested retail price $11.95**

Porter
Fifth in the Classic Beer Style Series

In the mid-18th century, porter was such a popular beer style that some of the fermenting vats were large enough for 100 to 200 people to dine in them during their inauguration. But more recently, this style was almost lost to modern beerlovers. Today porter is making a comeback, and Terry Foster brings to homebrewers the history, techniques and lore of this rich brew. Porter is the only book available on the style, and it is one of the most colorfully written and enjoyable beer style books available.

5 1/2 x 8 1/2, 142 pp.   **Suggested retail price $11.95**

Belgian Ale
Sixth in the Classic Beer Style Series

Discover the amazing complexity of Belgian ale with Pierre Rajotte. His passion for unique, flavorful beers has led him on a lifetime journey and taken him around the world in search of the ultimate brew. Follow along as Rajotte takes you on a journey of discovery in Belgium. Learn how Belgium's ethnic diversity has spawned more than 600 brands of beer. Rajotte teaches the importance of sugar, Belgian hops and top fermenting yeasts in the Belgian ale tradition. After reading *Belgian Ale* you'll be ready to brew your own Belgian-style, high gravity beer.

5 1/2 x 8 1/2, 176 pp.   **Suggested retail price $11.95**

German Wheat Beer
Seventh in the Classic Beer Style Series

Let Eric Warner, graduate of the prestigious Weihenstephan school of brewing in Germany, guide you through the history, tradition and profiles of wheat beer in this the most thoroughly written and researched book on the subject yet published. Warner, whose German-style Weizen took first place in the wheat beer category at the American Homebrewers Association 1992 National Homebrew Competition, offers readers an in depth look at this unique beer style. From history and profiles of original wheat beer recipes, to modern recipes and techniques fit for home or microbrewery use, Warner's *German Wheat Beer* answers all the questions.

5 1/2 x 8 1/2, approx. 160 pp.   **Suggested retail price $11.95**

Scotch Ale
Eighth in the Classic Beer Style Series

Learn the complete story, from conception through modern brewing techniques, with Greg Noonan's *Scotch Ale*. Noonan, author of ***Brewing Lager Beer*** (Brewers Publications, 1986) and owner and brewer of The Vermont Pub and Brewery of Burlington tells you all you need to know to brew this strong, dark, creamy beer. Since 1989 Noonan has brewed Scotch ale at The Vermont Pub and Brewery and has researched its profiles, history and recipes with the help of his wife's family of traditional Scotch brewers. If you want to brew this rich, traditional ale according to style, then Noonan's *Scotch Ale* has the information you need.

5 1/2 x 8 1/2, approx. 155 pp.   **Suggested retail price $11.95**